Productive Struggle in the K–5 Classroom

In today's world of being able to find answers at the click of a button, students need to learn how to grapple with complex concepts. But when is that struggle actually productive, and when is it just frustrating or discouraging? In this important book, bestselling author Barbara R. Blackburn shows how to help elementary students tackle hard topics in ways that will truly aid their learning.

You'll learn how productive struggle is connected to intrinsic motivation and how to scaffold instruction so you're not just throwing students into the deep end. You'll also find out how to pick the appropriate level of struggle and how to scaffold learning for students. Throughout, there are tons of practical charts, rubrics, and examples across subject areas, along with reflection questions to help you apply what you've learned. Bonus: Each chapter has a QR Code that takes you to related videos and additional tools.

With this highly practical guide, you'll be able to help students enjoy the fulfillment, confidence, and growth that comes with working through a challenging learning process.

Barbara R. Blackburn, a Top 30 Global Guru in Education, is the bestselling author of over 40 books and is a sought-after national and international consultant. She was an award-winning professor at Winthrop University and has taught early childhood, elementary, middle, and high school students.

Productive Struggle in the K–5 Classroom

Strategies Across the Content Areas

Barbara R. Blackburn

Routledge
Taylor & Francis Group
NEW YORK AND LONDON

Designed cover image: Getty Images

First published 2026
by Routledge
605 Third Avenue, New York, NY 10158

and by Routledge
4 Park Square, Milton Park, Abingdon, Oxon, OX14 4RN

Routledge is an imprint of the Taylor & Francis Group, an informa business

© 2026 Barbara R. Blackburn

The right of Barbara R. Blackburn to be identified as author of this work has been asserted in accordance with sections 77 and 78 of the Copyright, Designs and Patents Act 1988.

All rights reserved. No part of this book may be reprinted or reproduced or utilised in any form or by any electronic, mechanical, or other means, now known or hereafter invented, including photocopying and recording, or in any information storage or retrieval system, without permission in writing from the publishers.

Trademark notice: Product or corporate names may be trademarks or registered trademarks, and are used only for identification and explanation without intent to infringe.

For Product Safety Concerns and Information please contact our EU representative GPSR@taylorandfrancis.com. Taylor & Francis Verlag GmbH, Kaufingerstraße 24, 80331 München, Germany.

ISBN: 978-1-041-15455-6 (hbk)
ISBN: 978-1-041-15456-3 (pbk)
ISBN: 978-1-003-67952-3 (ebk)

DOI: 10.4324/9781003679523

Typeset in Palatino
by Apex CoVantage, LLC

Access the Support Material: Routledge.com/9781041154563

Support Material

The following tools from the book are also available on our website as free downloads, so you can easily print and reproduce them for classroom use. To access the materials, go to the book product page at www.Routledge.com/9781041154563 and click on the link that says Support Material.

Frustration Anchor Chart

Anchor Chart Primary Source Documents

Rubric for Teacher Behaviors

Rubric for Student Behaviors

Chart for Determining if Text is Too Hard

Explanation vs Justification

Academic Conversations Expectations

How to Get Help

Toolbox Check

Rescue Request

I dedicate this book to Lauren Davis, my editor for over 15 years and now also my publisher. She encourages, coaches, and inspires, and helps me be the best writer I can be. She is more than my editor and publisher—she is my dear friend.

Contents

Acknowledgments xi
Meet the Author xiii

Introduction 1

1 The Basics of Productive Struggle 3

2 Student Motivation and Learning Dispositions 17

3 Instruction for Productive Struggle 37

4 What Is the Right Level for Productive Struggle? 73

5 Scaffolding for Productive Struggle 91

6 Assessment in the Productive Struggle Classroom 139

7 Common Concerns About Productive Struggle 171

8 Collaborating for Productive Struggle 185

Bibliography 197

Acknowledgments

For my husband, Pete, who has the biggest heart of anyone I know.

For my mom, who, even with her Alzheimer's, always provides me a glimpse of hope!

For Darrin Parker, whose strength amazes me.

For Missy Miles, whose creativity as a teacher inspires me.

For Brad Witzel, who helped me refine my thoughts about the basis for productive struggle.

For the leaders and teachers at Freedom Middle School in Tennessee, I respect your commitment to growth—both your own and your students'.

Dr. Katie Perez for her fabulous Productive Struggle chart.

Emma Capel continues to design outstanding covers for my books.

Autumn Spalding's support in production makes my books come to life.

For the teachers and leaders both here in the United States and around the world (shout out to Australia), I admire your love for your students and your dedication to help them learn.

Meet the Author

Barbara R. Blackburn

Ranked in the Top 30 Global Gurus in Education, Barbara has dedicated her life to raising the level of expectation and motivation for professional educators and students alike. What differentiates Barbara's approximately 40 books are her easily executable concrete examples based on decades of experience as a teacher, professor, and consultant. Barbara's dedication to education was inspired in her early years by her parents, Bob and Rose. Her father's doctorate and lifetime career as a professor taught her the importance of professional training. Her mother's career as school secretary shaped Barbara's appreciation of the effort all staff play in the education of every child.

Barbara has taught early childhood, elementary, middle, and high school students and has served as an educational consultant for three publishing companies. She holds a master's degree in school administration and was certified as both a teacher and a school principal in North Carolina. She received her PhD in curriculum and teaching from the University of North Carolina at Greensboro. In 2006, she received the award for Outstanding Junior Professor at Winthrop University. She left her position at the University of North Carolina at Charlotte to write and speak full time.

In addition to speaking at state, national, and international conferences, she also regularly presents virtual and on-site workshops for teachers and administrators in elementary, middle, and high schools across the world. Her workshops are lively and engaging and filled with practical information. Topics include productive struggle, high expectations, scaffolding for support, instructional strategies, and leadership.

Introduction

I became intrigued by the notion of productive struggle several years ago. When I was a teacher, my students didn't want to do any work that required . . . well, work! They only wanted things that were easy. Over time, I was able to convince them that struggling to learn at higher levels was normal, and even positive. But it was a challenge, and some remained resistant. After I left my job as a teacher, I became an educational consultant and found that many other teachers faced the same situation. For many students, "harder work" was just hard. Later, when I accepted a job teaching graduate students at a university, my students asked me why students were so resistant to more challenging work. So I turned my attention to the topic of rigor and what that would look like in the classroom.

However, the issue of how to convince students to persist with challenging tasks continued to face teachers I worked with. A continuing question from teachers across the world was: "How do I help my students be successful when they are facing struggling in learning?" As one Australian teacher said, "Can struggle ever be productive?"

That's the question I answer in this book. First, let's set some parameters. Productive struggle is an opportunity for students to participate in a structured instructional situation in which they adapt current knowledge to solve a novel problem. Notice it is a structured situation. You don't just throw students into a task and allow them to struggle. Productive struggle occurs when it is a part of overall instruction. A piece of the puzzle is scaffolding. There will be times you will need to provide support for students, and that is acceptable. You just won't do the work for them.

There is some discussion on the difference between scaffolded complexity and scaffolded struggle. Scaffolded complexity focuses on increasing the complexity of content, skills, and tasks while scaffolded struggle is pointed toward the productive learning struggle itself. Although I do not use these terms, you will find that I discuss how to scaffold the content and how to scaffold the process, especially the dispositions needed for productive struggle.

Students also take what they know and use it to solve something new. Connections are key. We learn best when we build on a base, and that's what productive struggle does.

I'd like to take a moment to address how I used artificial intelligence in my writing. I was originally very reluctant to use any AI tools, but over time, I have learned that if I take what is in my head and use it to build a prompt, Chat GPT can help spark ideas for me. Throughout the book, I used it to help me build examples for a variety of subjects and grade levels. There were also times it helped me build a set of student responses. Please note I created the specific parameters of what I was looking for so it could generate an effective response. I then took the content and wrote it in my own words. While I didn't use it for the actual writing, I wanted to be transparent about finding it to be a helpful brainstorming tool for finding ideas in various areas.

I always view books as a journey—one in which you visit different aspects of a topic and learn from each. That's what I strive to provide for you. You'll find practical examples throughout the book, and questions that allow you to process your learning. I'd love to hear your experiences, if you'd like to share both the exciting examples and the frustrating ones. You can contact me with those or with questions through my website, drblackburn.us. Enjoy your journey!

1
The Basics of Productive Struggle

Introduction

One day, I was discussing education with my dad. He told me the best definition of the purpose of education he ever heard came from a third grade teacher. She said, "the purpose of education is for students to learn what to do when they don't know what to do." My dad explained that to him, it perfectly sums up learning. If you think about it, almost everything we do requires us to figure out what to do when we don't know what to do. Start a new job? Figure out what to do. Car breaks down? Solve the problem. Decide what to do after graduation? Determine what to do next.

That third-grade teacher's definition describes school, work, and life. And for us, it encapsulates the heart of productive struggle. Practicing how to struggle through a new learning situation is exactly what prepares us for the future.

In this chapter, we'll begin by looking at myths related to productive struggle, define productive struggle, and turn our attention to the rationale for including productive struggle in our classroom. Then, we'll examine the research base and the philosophical base for productive struggle. We'll finish with a road map for the remainder of this book.

> Myths
> Definition
> Rationale
> Research Base
> Philosophical Base
> Road Map

Myths Related to Productive Struggle

Too often, we have misconceptions about productive struggle. I spoke with one researcher who said, "There's nothing good about productive struggle. You're just being mean and punishing students with hard work." I understood his perspective—productive struggle can be misused or used inappropriately. Let's look at five key myths about productive struggle.

1. Productive struggle only is for the math classroom.
2. Students don't need any prior knowledge for productive struggle.
3. Students should struggle forever with no support.
4. There is no need to plan for productive struggle.
5. The harder the struggle, the better.

Productive Struggle Is Only for the Math Classroom

First, productive struggle is appropriate for any learning classroom, from the very youngest ages to the highest grade levels. It is also suitable for any subject area. You'll find examples throughout this book ranging from math and science to language arts and social studies to art, technology, and physical education. This myth tends to be popular because there has been an emphasis on productive struggle in the math classroom, especially through national standards.

Students Don't Need Any Prior Knowledge for Productive Struggle

Next, effective productive struggle opportunities build on students' prior knowledge. Students learn best when they can connect new knowledge to existing knowledge. In other words, "hooking" the old and new loops together is most effective. This is particularly true when they are struggling with learning.

Students Should Struggle Forever With No Support

This is probably the most dangerous myth. Struggle can be a positive part of learning, but too much struggle is detrimental to learning. This is true for all students, even your advanced learners. For example, I recently decided to learn a new hobby. I chose crochet, since my grandmother was a crocheter. I was doing well, then I hit a bump. I went back to the instructions but became more frustrated. Nothing I did worked. Then my husband suggested I ask for help from a Facebook group I'm in. Within an hour, I had four options to try and was immediately able to move forward. There's nothing effective about simply throwing students into an activity without support. The trick is to balance when you provide support, how much support you provide, and equipping students to ask for support only when needed. We'll explore this in Chapter 5.

There Is No Need to Plan for Productive Struggle

Planning opportunities for productive struggle is critical. The most effective productive struggle learning experiences are carefully planned, crafting the levels and types of struggle available, equipping students with the scaffolding skills they can use when they struggle, and building in self-assessment and metacognitive opportunities for students. We'll be discussing the aspects of effective productive struggle in Chapters 3, 4, 5, and 6.

The Harder the Struggle, the Better

With productive struggle, we are looking at complexity more than just difficulty level. For example, it may be difficult to solve a math problem in which you multiple two six digit numbers. However, that's still basic computation. Creating an alternative to the Pythagorean Theorem is far more complex and requires much more thinking. We'll spend Chapter 4 discussing how to determine the appropriate level of struggle.

Defining Productive Struggle

As you can see from the myths, there are misconceptions related to productive struggle. Therefore, it's important for us to clearly understand what productive struggle is. First, let's turn our attention to the National Council of Teachers of Mathematics. Productive struggle is a part of their national standards. In their supporting research guide (2017, p. 72), they turn to Hiebert and Wearne (2003), who point out that students need to be "given opportunities to wrestle with mathematical situations that are problematic to them but within their reach."

Explore Learning, in "What is Productive Struggle?", frames the concept similarly, noting that when students master content, it leads to "deep conceptual understanding and procedural fluency that transfers to new situations and persists over time."

In *Examining Productive Failure, Productive Success, Unproductive Failure, and Unproductive Success in Learning*, Manu Kapur points out that "productive success involves structuring problem solving and learning activities with the goal of achieving both improved performance on problem solving and sustainable learning" (p. 289).

Tom Thibodeau in *What is Productive Struggle* (2024) explains that productive struggle is a concept best described as a person's ability to work through a problem to find a solution or complete a task (par. 2). Getting it isn't always easy, but in reality, learning will be more profound if our students have to work a bit harder to build their knowledge and skills. He also notes that productive struggle is not a new concept, which we'll discuss later in this chapter.

Finally, Jami Witherell, writing for the Goyen Institute in *Embracing Productive Struggle: Why Its Essential for Literacy Learning*, explains it simply (par. 4):

> Productive struggle happens when students face a challenge that's just tough enough to make them think, but not so hard that they shut down. It's that sweet spot where learning happens. It's when they push through the discomfort and find the solution on their own.

Let's look at the commonalities. First, all of the examples focus on learning, particularly new situations. Second, appropriate struggle is inherent in the process. Third, implied throughout the definitions is that the learning situation is planned.

As I've worked with productive struggle, I've found we can use a clear, thorough, teacher-friendly definition as we move forward.

> Productive struggle is an opportunity for students to participate in a structured instructional situation in which they adapt current knowledge to solve a novel problem.

There are several key words and phrases in my definition. First is student participation. You simply can't have productive struggle without students participating in the process. Next, it is a structured instructional situation. Generally, teachers plan and craft the opportunity for students to apply prior knowledge in a new situation at a level which requires the right level of struggle—not too little, not too much. We'll address this in Chapter 4. Finally, students are using the knowledge they already have, just to something that is new to them. Connecting the two is an intricate part of productive struggle.

Why Is Productive Struggle Important?

There are four broad reasons to incorporate productive struggle in our instruction.

> **Rationale for Productive Struggle**
> 1. strengthen learning;
> 2. enhance the brain;
> 3. improve social and emotional skills;
> 4. prepare to work.

Strengthen Learning

As we explore how productive struggle impacts your classroom, it's important to realize that it strengthens student learning. Not only can it promote retention, it can also deepen overall understanding (Sriram, 2020). Additionally, Manu Kapur explains that there is a "growing body of evidence that generating solutions to novel problems prior to instruction can help students learn better from the instruction" (p. 292).

> **Sample Research**
>
> *Quasiexperimental Studies*
>
> Schwartz & Bransford, 1998
> Schwartz & Martin, 2004
>
> *Controlled Experimental Studies*
>
> DeCaro & Rittle-Johnson, 2012
> Loibl & Rummel, 2013, 2014
> Roll, Aleven, & Koedinger, 2011
> R. A. Schmidt & Bjork, 1992
> Schwartz, Chase, Oppezzo, & Chin, 2011

Enhance the Brain

There are several ways the brain is impacted by productive struggle. The staff at ST Math explain that "our brains are designed to adapt and grow through challenges." Difficult tasks such as productive struggle strengthen neural connections and enhance cognitive abilities. Rishi Sriram (2020) shares four specific brain benefits of productive struggle.

1. Building stronger neural pathways. The more a student struggles in a healthy way and overcomes challenges, the stronger these pathways become. Neuroplasticity, is how our brains grow and adapt.
2. Engaging working memory. Productive struggle taps into working memory (holds and processes info ono the spot). When students are faced with a literacy task just beyond their comfort zone, they're forced to pull from what they already know, apply that knowledge, and then make sense of the new information.
3. Gaining a dopamine reward. Overcoming a challenge releases dopamine in the brain (feel good chemical).
4. Encoding for long-term learning. When students struggle productively, their brains work harder to encode that information into long-term memory

Improve Social and Emotional Skills

Productive struggle can also improve students' social and emotional skills. For example, *Effortful Practice* authors explain that productive struggle helps students with goal-setting, planning of strategies, and monitoring their own progress, which includes students knowing when and how to ask for help. Additionally, Ellie Cowen (2016) shares that perseverance and effort are a key part of productive struggle. Finally, Rishi Sriram (2020) notes that both resilience and growth mindset can expand with productive struggle. We will address all these areas in more depth in Chapter 2.

Prepare to Work

Productive struggle can also help prepare students for the workforce. Simply moving into the workforce is a struggle for many students, so having practiced that skill is helpful. For example, according to the UK Editorial Board at Indeed, an international job search site, struggles may include time management, collaboration, work-life balance and communication (https://uk.indeed.com/career-advice/career-development/struggle-at-work). When students engage in productive struggle, they must manage their time and effectively communicate and collaborate with other students.

For their 2025 Future of Jobs Report (https://reports.weforum.org/docs/WEF_Future_of_Jobs_Report_2025.pdf), the World Economic Forum's surveyed 100 of the largest employers in the world. Four of their top ten ranked workforce skills can be a regular part of productive struggle, especially when you craft effective opportunities.

> #4 creative thinking;
> #5 resilience, flexibility, and agility;
> #6 curiosity;
> #9 analytical thinking.

The World Economic Forum also noted that 39% of the key skills required for work will change by 2030. In other words, many key work skills don't even exist today for current sixth graders.

What Is the Research Base for Productive Struggle?

There is some discussion as to how much research supports productive struggle. Although there is not a large base of research specific to the strategy of productive strategy, we can be informed by research on the elements of productive struggle, which we will discuss in more detail in Chapter 3. My "go-to" for research is the bank of meta-analyses by John Hattie (https://visible-learning.org/hattie-ranking-influences-effect-sizes-learning-achievement/). John synthesizes research studies to identify practices that make the most impact on students.

In his newest work, John Hattie with Douglas Fisher et al. (2024) classifies the rankings from his meta-analyses using the analogy of a thermometer. Effect sizes lower than 0 are "cold," meaning they have a negative impact on achievement. Effect sizes from 0–0.4 are "cool," or they positively affect achievement. Finally, those .5 or above are "hot," which represents effects with above average impact.

Using John's work, I've divided identified effective research practice strategies into two categories: practices the teacher drives, and those in which the students participate and are responsible for. I've provided the practice, and the effect size. These are grouped by similarities rather than effect size.

Teacher Practices and Student Responsibilities

Teacher Practices	Students' Responsibilities
.9 teacher expectations high for all	.77 effort
.85 teacher clarity	.75 evaluation and reflection
.64 organization of instruction	.56 concentration, persistence, engagement
.68 learning goals	.48 questioning
.59 appropriately challenging goals	1.23 student expectations
.64 interpretations based on assessment of student learning	.75 elaboration and organization
	.59 elaborative interrogation
	.54 strategy monitoring
.88 ensure students understand the criteria of success	.81 self-judgement and reflection
.93 integration with prior knowledge	.52 meta-cognitive strategies
.94 prior ability	.85 organizing and transforming notes
.96 teaching students to drive their learning	.74 reciprocal teaching
.47 small group	.5 study skills
.82 class discussion	.82 classroom discussion
.5 inquiry based teaching	.62 concept mapping
.92 constructivist teaching	.58 self-verbalization and self-questioning
.44 inductive teaching	
.29 cognitive task analysis	.45 collaborative learning
.68 problem solving teaching	.62 graphic organizers and concept maps
.52 self-regulation learning	
.82 scaffolding	
.46 providing examples and guided practice	

Teacher practices of having appropriately challenging goals, integrating prior knowledge, using constructivist teaching, and problem-solving teaching all lend themselves to a lesson that incorporates productive struggle. For students, using effort, evaluation and reflection, and collaborative learning support productive learning. Both these teacher and student examples, as well as the other in the table, can be used in other aspects of classroom instruction, but they are particularly pertinent with productive struggle. Again, we'll be looking at these in more detail in Chapter 3.

What Is the Philosophical Base for Productive Struggle?

The field of education has a wide range of educational philosophers. When I was in college, I was required to write my own philosophy, based on other philosophies. I ultimately synthesized parts of existing philosophies and added my own perspective. Although I've added in new pieces, my philosophy today is still reflective of that writing. When researching productive struggle, I went back to that process. I reviewed educational philosophers and pulled the aspects that support productive struggle. In this section, you'll find that productive struggle is representative of a variety of philosophers in education. My source for this entire section is *Learning Theories Simplified . . . and How to Apply Them to Teaching*, third edition by Bob Bates. I highly recommend the book as a comprehensive source of information about educational philosophers.

Educational Philosophers

Jean-Jacques Rousseau
Jean Piaget
Jerome Bruner
John Dewey
Paolo Freire
Edward Tolman
Lev Vygostsky
Norman Doidge
Renate and Geoffrey Caine
Logan Fiorella and Richard E. Mayer
Barak Rosenshine
Leslie Curzon

> Carol Dweck
> Michael Shayer and Phillip Adey
> Robin Alexander

For example, from Jean-Jacques Rousseau we find that people should be able to learn what they want to learn and that teaching should be based on discovery enriched with the teacher guidance.

In addition to his four stages of development, Jean Piaget also posits that learners should be encouraged to learn from their peers and that learners should be allowed to learn from their mistakes. Learning from mistakes is especially important in productive struggle.

Jerome Bruner continues the focus on learning. He specifically recommends that students are allowed to discover new material to be covered so they can connect with their own understanding. This points to the very nature of discovery learning in productive struggle.

Next, John Dewey teaches us that, rather than communicating knowledge and skills but the role of a teacher is to use their learner's experiences as a teaching tool. Additionally, the challenge in providing experience-based lessons is to provide quality experiences that result in creativity and growth. Teachers must also provide guidance to learners in their use of observation and judgment. Each of these recommendations supports our use of productive struggle.

Paulo Freire gives us the concept of critical consciousness. The five step process is helpful as we develop situations for productive struggle.

> 1. identify the problem;
> 2. find an original way of representing the problem;
> 3. see the problem through your learner's eyes;
> 4. analyze the cause of the problem;
> 5. take action to solve the problem.

One of Edward Tolman's key principles is that learning is always purposeful and goal directed. That's important because students typically don't apply their learning unless they have a reason to do so. During productive struggle, the natural result is that students apply their learning.

Lev Vygotsky provides a key idea related to productive struggle: learning occurs in the zone of proximal development, the optimal level of difficulty. We will focus on this in Chapter 4.

Norman Doidge builds on the work of Vygotsky's level of challenge. He discusses the considering the concept of brain plasticity in order to ensure teaching has the right balance of challenge and support.

Renate and Geoffrey Caine point out the brain is a living system. Learning is enhanced by challenge, but is inhibited by threat, therefore it is critical to provide the right level of challenge in students' opportunities for productive struggle.

Logan Fiorella and Richard E. Mayer promote 8 learning strategies under the framework of the Generative Learning Theory. All of these are useful as students are working through the process of productive struggle.

Eight Learning Strategies

1. learning by summarizing;
2. learning by mapping;
3. learning by drawing;
4. learning by imagining;
5. learning by self-testing;
6. learning by self-explaining;
7. learning by teaching;
8. learning by enacting.

Barak Rosenshine notes two crucial aspects that are essential to productive struggle: Have high expectations of your students and provide scaffolding for difficult tasks.

Leslie Curzon fleshes out our philosophy by discussing motivation. If we set goals for students that are too hard or too easy, we undermine motivation (Chapter 2).

Carol Dweck added to the philosophical base when she posited that there is a difference between a fixed mindset and a growth mindset. Students with a fixed mindset believe they are smart or not and cannot change. On the other hand, students with a growth mindset believe that, with effort, they can change and grow. A growth mindset is essential to productive struggle.

Michael Shayer and Phillip Adey detail the concept of cognitive acceleration. As we consider productive struggle, notice how these points reinforce productive struggle that promotes student learning.

Cognitive Acceleration

- If learners are given a challenge without preparation they will fail the task.
- If teachers give the answers learners may remember the facts.

> - If learners develop the answers themselves they will understand.
> - If learners are then encouraged to discuss how they could apply their thinking process. they have undertaken to other areas, then they "become cleverer."

Finally, Robin Alexander's extensive writings demonstrate the effectiveness of dialogue in the classroom. She also focuses on working in groups and building on other students' ideas. Each of these are aspects of effective productive struggle.

Road Map to Book

I always consider reading a book to be a journey . . . a journey of learning. As we move forward, we'll be exploring the following areas.

	Areas to Explore
Chapter 2: Student Motivation and Learning Dispositions	We'll focus on student motivation, especially intrinsic motivation, and then turn to the learning dispositions students display during productive struggle.
Chapter 3: Instruction for Productive Struggle	With a focus on instruction, we'll address general principles, the before-during-after process of instruction, and teacher and student behaviors for productive struggle.
Chapter 4: What is the Right Level for Productive Struggle?	In addition to discussing Vygotsky and Csikszentmihalyi, we'll look at leveled texts and a variety of appropriately leveled productive struggle tasks.
Chapter 5: Scaffolding for Productive Struggle	Filled with suggestions for general scaffolding, this chapter also revisits tasks from Chapter 4 and adds appropriate scaffolding suggestions.

Areas to Explore	
Chapter 6: Assessment in the Productive Struggle Classroom	We'll explore formative and summative assessment for the process of productive struggle, then turn our attention to formative and summative assessment for the content of productive struggle.
Chapter 7: Common Concerns about Productive Struggle	We'll address the issues of working with special needs students, learned helplessness, communicating with parents and families, and organizing for productive struggle.
Chapter 8: Collaborating for Productive Struggle	We'll discuss ways teachers can work together to consistently implement productive struggle in their classrooms.

A Final Note

Although there are many myths about productive struggle, ultimately, productive struggle is an opportunity for students to participate in a structured instructional situation in which they adapt current knowledge to solve a novel problem. There is both a research base and a philosophical foundation for incorporating productive struggle in your classroom.

Points to Ponder

1. Which myth resonates with you? Why?
2. How did you respond when you read the definition of productive struggle?
3. Which parts of the research base match what you do in your classroom?
4. What aspects of the philosophical foundation do you agree with?

Continue the Learning

Use the QR Code to access videos for your own use or for group professional development.

2
Student Motivation and Learning Dispositions

Now that we've looked at the overall base of information related to productive struggle, we need to turn our attention to two areas that are critically connected: student motivation and learning dispositions.

Many teachers tell me, "my students just aren't motivated," which is a major concern for productive struggle. After all, if students aren't motivated now, how will you convince them to attempt to do work that requires struggle? If you've read *Motivating Struggling Learners: 10 Strategies to Build Student Success*, you know that I believe all students are motivated, just not necessarily by the things we would like. Many of our students are not motivated by a desire to learn; rather, they are motivated by the approval of their friends or something else in their lives. As we start this chapter, we're going to briefly address extrinsic motivation, then turn our attention to intrinsic motivation.

Motivation

Extrinsic and Intrinsic Motivation

There are two main types of motivation: extrinsic and intrinsic. Extrinsic motivation includes all the outside ways we try to influence a student, such as rewards, stickers, or points. Intrinsic motivation comes from within the student. With extrinsic rewards, we can get temporary results, but for long-term impact, we need to help students activate their intrinsic motivation.

It's similar to looking at the ocean. I enjoy watching the waves, but when doing so I only sees the surface. I can't see the perilous undercurrents. Similarly, extrinsic motivation looks good, but we don't notice the dangers. The true beauty of the ocean is underneath the surface. As we go deeper there are beautiful marine creatures, fish, and coral. Instead of short-lived waves, I can see long-lasting beauty. And that is intrinsic motivation.

Extrinsic Motivation

Extrinsic motivation is that which comes from outside a student; anything that is external.

> **Examples of Extrinsic Rewards**
> Points
> Stickers
> Grades
> Library or homework passes
> Candy/toys
> Smiley faces
> Extra credit

Positive Aspects of Extrinsic Motivation

Some authors, such as Alfie Kohn, believe there is never an appropriate use for external motivation, whether for children or students. Based on my experiences, I believe there are appropriate uses for it. For example, I agree with Daniel Pink, author of *Drive*, who compares extrinsic motivation to caffeine, noting it gets you going (although you are less motivated later). Especially when students are beginning the process of productive struggle, extrinsic may be a good jumpstart.

Larry Ferlazzo in *Self-Driven Learning* also points out that everyone needs some baseline rewards, such as a clean classroom, a caring student, engaging lessons, and fair grading, in order to be motivated to learn. And Daniel Pink also points out that extrinsic rewards do work for a short time for mechanical, rote tasks, which may be needed prior to productive struggle activities.

Negative Aspects of Extrinsic Motivation

> **Negative Aspects of Extrinsic Motivation**
> Temporary/constant increase of reward
> Decreases intrinsic motivation

There is, however, a downside to extrinsic motivation. The results are most often temporary. To keep students motivated, while relying on extrinsic motivation, you must continue to increase the reward. A student I spoke with explained "I had a reward box where students could choose an item if they did something good. Over time, students wanted more and more . . . stickers weren't enough, then points weren't enough, then books weren't enough, etc."

Effective Ways to Use Extrinsic Motivation

"But," you may be thinking, "my students expect rewards. I can't just not use them!" So how can you effectively use extrinsic rewards? I think it's important to go back to Larry Ferlazzo's comments about baseline rewards. For all students, we need to provide:

- a clean, safe, caring environment;
- adequate materials and supplies;
- clear and fair instruction;
- openness to all ideas and suggestions.

It's important to address those areas during productive struggle. In addition, when using extrinsic rewards, we should emphasize the feeling that accompanies the reward, reinforcing that the true reward is how you feel about your success. In other words, move from a reward to celebrating the experience.

There are three other specific tips for using extrinsic motivation. First, when using rewards, do so unannounced. Rather than saying "if then, then this," simply choose random times to reward students. By surprising students, they are encouraged to put forth effort all the time.

Next, reward students through affirmation of their work. Give them an authentic audience who can appreciate their quality work.

Third, when you are using rewards, make them appropriate and meaningful to the student. Some students like certificates; others prefer public recognition. It's also important to be respectful of the individual. Some students do not like to be singled out in front of their peers. If you know that, find another way to praise them: a note, an individual comment, or even a look.

Intrinsic Motivation

Intrinsic motivation is that which comes from within the student. It is internal as opposed to external. With intrinsic motivation, students appreciate learning for its own sake. They enjoy learning and the feelings of accomplishment that accompany the activity, and that is key to productive struggle. There are many benefits to intrinsic motivation.

The Foundational Elements of Intrinsic Motivation

Intrinsic motivation has two foundational elements: People are more motivated when they value what they are doing and when they believe they have a chance for success. Students see value in a variety of ways, but the main three are relevance, autonomy, and relationships.

Value

Students typically see value through the relevance of the tasks they are asked to do, whether that is completing a word problem that includes their dogs, or understanding how the lesson is related to a hobby, such as skateboarding. In fact, most students have a streaming music station playing in their heads, WII-FM—what's in it for me? As you develop tasks and activities for productive struggle, you'll want to think about the relevance of what students are doing. When students do see value in their learning, they are more motivated to push through when the work requires struggle.

Next, there is value in the autonomy a student has. I've talked to students who say, "I'm told what to do, how to do it, and when to do it! I'm a student and I know what I am doing. When do I get to decide something?" That is actually a fairly common perception from students. Although there are some non-negotiables you deal with, if you will find options for students to make decisions, you can encourage autonomy and intrinsic motivation.

Ways to Increase Student Autonomy During Productive Struggle

Offer choice of books and resources

Give different ways to complete the productive struggle task

Agree to students' views on how to demonstrate understanding

Allow options of what to do when students finish their work

Provide opportunities for students to choose partners

Finally, students find value in their relationships, with you and their peers. I once heard a speaker say that teacher and peer relationships are foundational to everything else that happens in the school. That is true. The old adage, "they don't care what you know until they know how much you care" is true. Students need to feel liked, cared for, and respected by their leaders. Many students also need the same from their peers. If they feel isolated from other students, they are disengaged and less likely to see value in what they are doing.

Success

Students are also motivated when they believe they have a chance to be successful. And that belief is built on four building blocks: level of challenge, experiences, encouragement, and views about success.

First, the degree of alignment between the difficulty of an activity and a student's skill level is a major factor in self-motivation. Imagine that you enjoy playing soccer, and you have the chance to compete in a local game. You will be playing against Lionel Messi (Miami), named World Player of the Year a record eight times. How do you feel? In that situation, there's plenty of opportunity for challenge, probably too much challenge! Or perhaps you love reading stories, but the only language you can read is Spanish. How motivated will you be in a literature class? For optimal motivation, the activity should be challenging but in balance with your ability to perform. Part of your job as a teacher is to determine if a student is struggling, and if so, provide appropriate support. On the other hand, if one of your students is not challenged, look for ways to give them an opportunity to try a new challenge. Productive struggle is the perfect way to provide challenge, and we'll spend Chapter 4 discussing how to determine the right level of challenge.

A student's experiences are an important factor to their success with productive struggle. A student is more likely to believe they can be successful if they have been successful in the past. Conversely, if they have a pattern of failing, they will struggle with motivation.

A third building block to feelings of success is the encouragement a student receives from others. Encouragement is "the process of facilitating the development of the person's inner resources and courage towards positive movement" (Dinkmeyer & Losoncy, 1992, p. 16).

When you encourage, you accept students as they are, so they will accept themselves. You value and reinforce attempts and efforts and help them realize that mistakes are learning tools. Encouragement says, "Try, and try again. You can do it. Go in your own direction, at your own pace. I believe in you." Encouragement can be in the form of words, but you can also provide encouragement through a consistent, positive presence in your students' lives.

Planning for Motivation	
Aspect of Intrinsic Motivation	*How I'll Build This Into Productive Struggle*
Value: relevance	
Value: autonomy	
Value: relationships	
Success: challenge	
Success: experiences	
Success: encouragement	
Success: view	

It's also important for students to read and learn about people who failed before they succeeded, because the final building block is a student's views about success and failure. Many students see failure as the end rather than as an opportunity to learn before trying again. But there are countless examples, from Abraham Lincoln to Steve Jobs, of people who have experienced failure in their lives, only to become successful. How we define success and failure drives many of your students' beliefs about your own ability to succeed.

Learning Dispositions

Now that we've discussed the broad concepts of motivation, I want us to turn our attention to the dispositions students display. As I researched productive struggle, it became clear that, which academic skills are critical, so are the learning dispositions that students have. These tend to fit under the broader concept of motivation. Although they are sometimes called thinking skills, soft skills, or non-academic skills, learning dispositions is a better descriptor for what we want. These are the mental attitudes and skills that students have (and can improve upon) that help them solve the problems that occur in productive struggle. First, let's review some related research, then discuss my five dispositions for productive struggle. That section will include practical strategies for encouraging each disposition in your classroom. Please note those are not productive struggle activities; they are activities which allow students to practice particular dispositions.

Related Research and Theories

Costa and Kallick

First, Arthur Costa and Bena Kallick (2008) address their perspective on Habits of Mind. These are dispositions for intelligent behavior and support problem-solving and lifelong learning. As they point out, their identified list is focused on "thinking dispositions, or tendencies toward particular patterns of intellectual behavior" (p. 19).

Sixteen Habits of Mind

1. persisting;
2. managing impulsivity;
3. listening with understanding and empathy;
4. thinking flexibly;
5. thinking about thinking (metacognition);
6. striving for accuracy;
7. questioning and posing problems;
8. applying past knowledge to new situations;
9. thinking and communicating with clarity and precision;
10. gathering data through all senses;
11. creating, imagining, innovating;
12. responding with wonderment and awe;
13. taking responsible risks;
14. finding humor;
15. thinking interdependently;
16. remaining open to continuous learning.

Claxton

Guy Claxton's Learning Power Approach (LPA) identifies mental ingredients that make up learning power, which can be built, just as muscle power can be built. As Guy points out, "the approach is to develop all students as confident and capable learners—ready, willing, and able to choose, design, research, pursue, troubleshoot, and evaluate learning for themselves, alone and with others, in school or out (p. 40)." His list also encompasses other embedded areas.

> Curiosity
> Attention
> Determination
> Imagination
> Thinking
> Socializing
> Reflection
> Organization

Wagner

Tony Wagner, the author of *The Global Achievement Gap* (2008) takes a different approach. He focuses on thinking skills that are necessary to survive in life, but particularly in the workforce. He considers the identified dispositions as survival skills. "Indeed, the 7 survival skills are for future generations what the 'Three Rs' were for previous generations. They are the 'new basic skills' for work, learning, and citizenship in the 21st century" (p. 42).

Seven Survival Skills

1. critical thinking and problem solving;
2. collaboration across networks and leading by influence;
3. agility and adaptability;
4. initiative and entrepreneurialism;
5. effective oral and written communication;
6. accessing and analyzing information;
7. curiosity and imagination.

Ritchhart

In 2002, Ron Ritchhart released a book on intellectual character. His main focus, that education should shape intellectual character, included information on using dispositions to build character, which will encourage critical and reflective thinking. As he describes it,

> What does intelligence look like in action? What are the qualities of thought and characteristics of mind we expect to see when someone is acting intelligently? What are the patterns of behavior and attitudes that we associate with someone who acts smart?
>
> (p. 13)

He notes that intelligence is not something you possess as much as how you perform. Dispositions are critical to that.

Dispositions

1. Creative thinking: looking out, up, around, and about
    - open-minded
    - curious
2. Reflective thinking: looking within
    - metacognitive
3. Critical thinking: looking at, through, and in between
    - seeking truth and understanding
    - strategic
    - skeptical

Australian Girls in STEM Toolkit

Finally, I turned to Australia for a different perspective, although one with common themes.

The Girls in STEM Toolkit (the GiST) focuses on providing girls and young women with resources to help them understand how their existing skills and interests can link to STEM careers and study pathways. Funded by the Australian Government Department of Industry, Science and Resources and managed by Education Services Australia, it provides a range of helpful tools for teachers.

Their work with dispositions is founded on the belief that having a growth mindset is important for girls to move forward with STEM studies and careers. Specific dispositions can be evidenced by behaviors in the classroom.

> - curiosity and scepticism (skepticism);
> - collaboration;
> - creativity;
> - persistence;
> - problem-solving;
> - intellectual risk-taking;
> - making connections.

https://www.thegist.edu.au/educators/create-inclusive-classrooms/talk-tools-build-stem-capital/foster-stem-dispositions/

Dispositions for Productive Struggle

Based on the previous information, I synthesized and coordinated the dispositions into a simple set of five general dispositions that are needed in a productive struggle classroom.

> Curiosity and Creative Thinking
> Persistence and Self-Discipline
> Strategic Problem-Solving and Metacognition
> Risk-Taking
> Integrating Thinking

You may be wondering why I didn't include collaboration in my list. I will address students' working together in Chapter 5, but I consider that to be more of a social skill than a disposition.

Let's look at each of these five in depth. I'll start by expanding on the disposition with more detail, share a picture of what the disposition looks like when students are starting to activate the disposition, beginning to master the disposition, then demonstrating skill with the disposition. I'll finish each section by providing a primary (K-2) and upper elementary (3–5) example of activities you can do in the classroom to foster the disposition.

Curiosity and Creative Thinking

Curiosity and creative thinking incorporates questioning, generating original ideas, and open-mindedness. This also includes that students evaluate information for bias or false information and act accordingly. In other words, they test possibilities through critical evaluation, looking for facts and evidence.

Measuring Up With Curiosity and Creative Thinking

Demonstrating Skill with the Disposition
Students generate new ideas, ask new and probing questions, are genuinely curious about learning, and seek out the truth for learning, particularly looking for evidence and the bias included.

Beginning to Master the Disposition
Students share new ideas, ask a variety of questions, are curious about some aspects of learning, and sometimes evaluate whether or not the information is true based on evidence.

Starting to Activate the Disposition
Students are beginning to share ideas, ask few questions, are sometimes curious about some aspects of learning, but rarely question the information learned or seek any evidence.

Generating Original Ideas Activity

> ### Kindergarten
>
> After studying traits of various animals, students must combine at least two traits to create a new animal.

> ### Grade Three
>
> Based on games they have played in physical education and during recess, groups create their own game and teach it to the rest of the class.

Looking for Bias Activity

> ### Grade Two
>
> After reading *The Three Little Pigs* and *The True Story of the Three Little Pigs*, choose another book. Then rewrite the story from a second character's perspective.

> ### Grade Five
>
> Look for bias in headlines. Find a variety of news headlines on the same topic (using a safe search engine is helpful). Analyze the headlines and discuss why some are worded differently.

Persistence and Self-discipline

With this disposition, students sustain effort throughout the productive learning process. They also manage their frustration when things are not going well.

Measuring Up With Persistence and Self-discipline

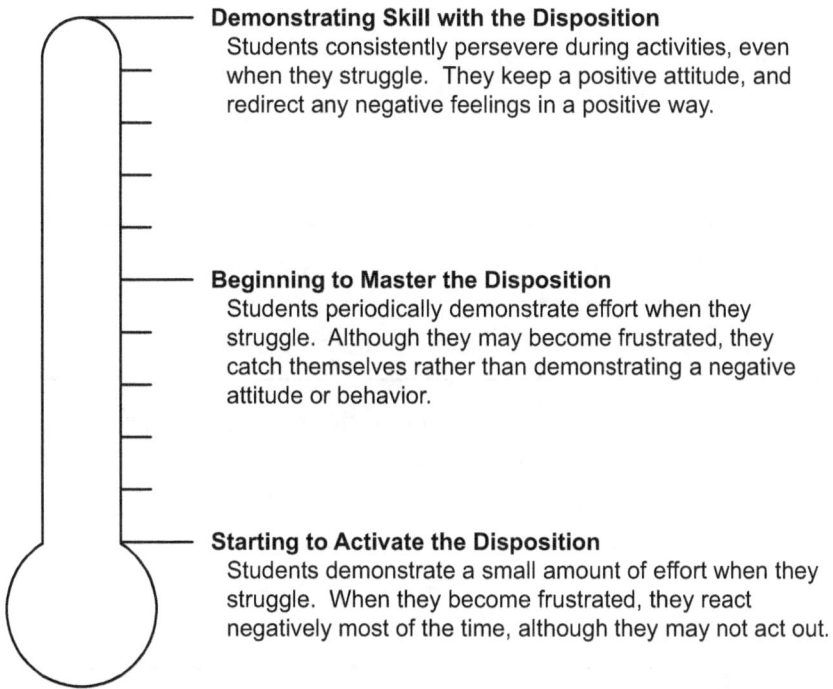

Demonstrating Skill with the Disposition
Students consistently persevere during activities, even when they struggle. They keep a positive attitude, and redirect any negative feelings in a positive way.

Beginning to Master the Disposition
Students periodically demonstrate effort when they struggle. Although they may become frustrated, they catch themselves rather than demonstrating a negative attitude or behavior.

Starting to Activate the Disposition
Students demonstrate a small amount of effort when they struggle. When they become frustrated, they react negatively most of the time, although they may not act out.

Showing Effort Activity

K-2

Ask students to draw a picture. You will explain each step, and tell them they may not get it right the first time. Then, walk them through the drawing step-by-step (draw a line straight down from the middle of the page). After they finish, discuss whether they had to put forth effort. Then, show them the original picture and let them adjust their drawing.

3–5

Give students a maze that has multiple tricky turns and dead ends. After the time is up, discuss how they handled and what strategies helped them keep going.

Managing Frustration Activity

Using an anchor chart similar to the two below adapted from Chat GPT, brainstorm ideas with students as to how they feel when they are frustrated and what they can do instead.

K-2 Version of Frustration Anchor Chart	
When I Feel Frustrated . . .	*I Can Try . . .*
I'm scared	Think of something positive
I want to stop	Remember a time you kept working
I don't know what to do	Ask someone for help
I get stuck	Think of another time you got stuck and then unstuck
It's hard	Take a deep breath and try again

3–5 Version of Frustration Anchor Chart	
When I Feel Frustrated . . .	*I Can Try . . .*
I feel tense or upset	Take 3 slow breaths or stretch my body
I want to quit	Remind myself: 'I can't do it YET, but I will keep trying.'
I'm stuck	Break the problem into smaller steps
I feel discouraged	Think of a time I solved a hard problem before
It's confusing	Try a new strategy or ask a specific question for help
I feel overwhelmed	Take a short break to calm down, then return

Strategic Problem-Solving and Metacognition

Students not only use problem solving and strategic thinking skills, they also reflect on their own thinking and make appropriate adjustments in order to be successful.

Measuring Up With Strategic Problem-Solving and Metacognition

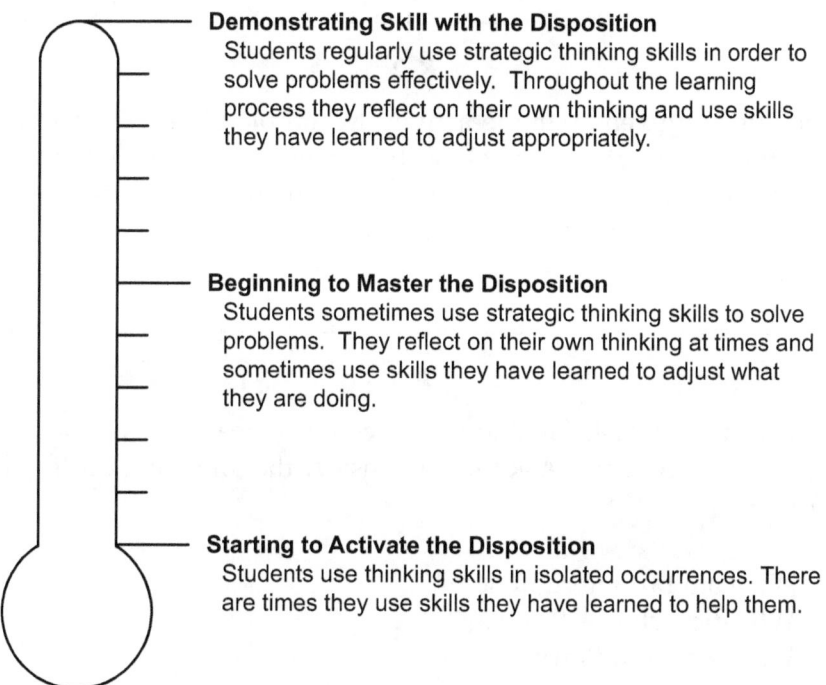

Demonstrating Skill with the Disposition
Students regularly use strategic thinking skills in order to solve problems effectively. Throughout the learning process they reflect on their own thinking and use skills they have learned to adjust appropriately.

Beginning to Master the Disposition
Students sometimes use strategic thinking skills to solve problems. They reflect on their own thinking at times and sometimes use skills they have learned to adjust what they are doing.

Starting to Activate the Disposition
Students use thinking skills in isolated occurrences. There are times they use skills they have learned to help them.

Problem-Solving Activity

Grade One
Groups of students build a tower that is taller than a pencil and will not fall using provided materials.

> **Grade Four**
>
> Solve the Mystery! The teacher provides a mystery, such as the missing lunch. Students look for clues, question suspects, and solve the mystery.

Metacognition Activity

> **K-2**
>
> Students are given a simple activity to complete. Ask them to use one "thinking strategy" they have been taught. Display these with a picture on an anchor chart. While completing the activity, they draw the appropriate picture where they use it.

> **3–5**
>
> Provide a short task for students. It could be reading, writing, or a set of math problems. Ask them to answer the following during the activity:
>
> - What am I trying right now?
> - Why did I choose this way?
> - What else could I try?

Risk-Taking

This area focuses on intellectual risk-taking. In other words, students ask questions, especially ones for which they do not know the answers. They also tolerate uncertainty and embrace mistakes as opportunities for growth.

Measuring Up With Risk-Taking

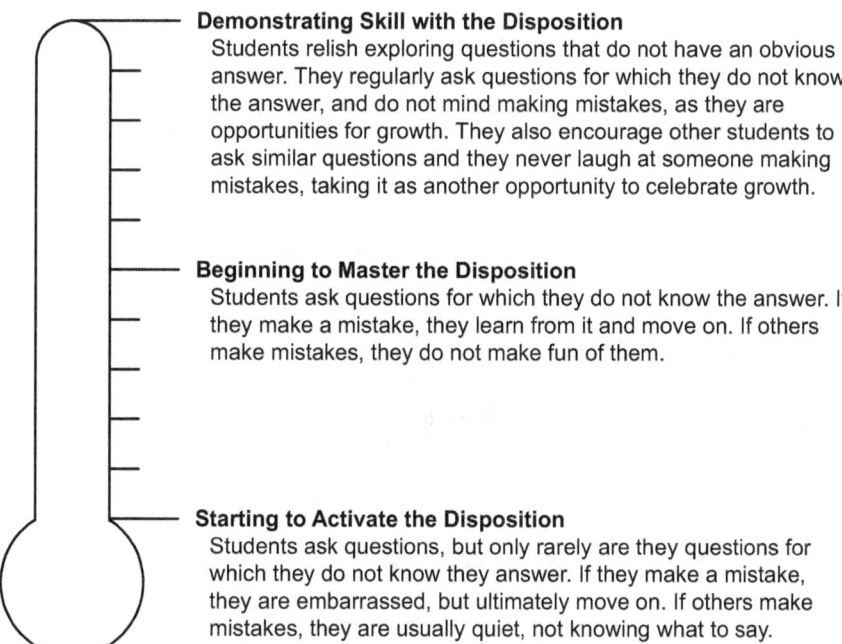

Demonstrating Skill with the Disposition
Students relish exploring questions that do not have an obvious answer. They regularly ask questions for which they do not know the answer, and do not mind making mistakes, as they are opportunities for growth. They also encourage other students to ask similar questions and they never laugh at someone making mistakes, taking it as another opportunity to celebrate growth.

Beginning to Master the Disposition
Students ask questions for which they do not know the answer. If they make a mistake, they learn from it and move on. If others make mistakes, they do not make fun of them.

Starting to Activate the Disposition
Students ask questions, but only rarely are they questions for which they do not know they answer. If they make a mistake, they are embarrassed, but ultimately move on. If others make mistakes, they are usually quiet, not knowing what to say.

Tolerating Uncertainty Activity

All Grades (Vary Items)

Mystery Box. Put a variety of items in a sealed box. Students write a story about the items without knowing what they are. Afterward, open the box, compare the stories and the items, but discuss how it felt to not know the items.

Uncertain Questions

You can use these questions for discussion or writing. Each is designed to be uncertain.

K-2 Questions

What do you think clouds would say if they could talk?
Which color is the most important, and why?
What would happen if it was nighttime all the time?
If you could trade places with a bird, what would you do first?
Is it better to go fast or slow? Why?

> ### 3–5 Questions
> Which is more powerful: words or actions?
> Is it possible to ever know everything?
> Which is more important: asking questions or finding answers?
> What does it mean to be free?
> Is change always good? Why or why not?

Integrating Thinking

Students apply their prior knowledge, make connections, and transfer learning across lessons, texts, and/or subjects.

Measuring Up With Integrating Thinking

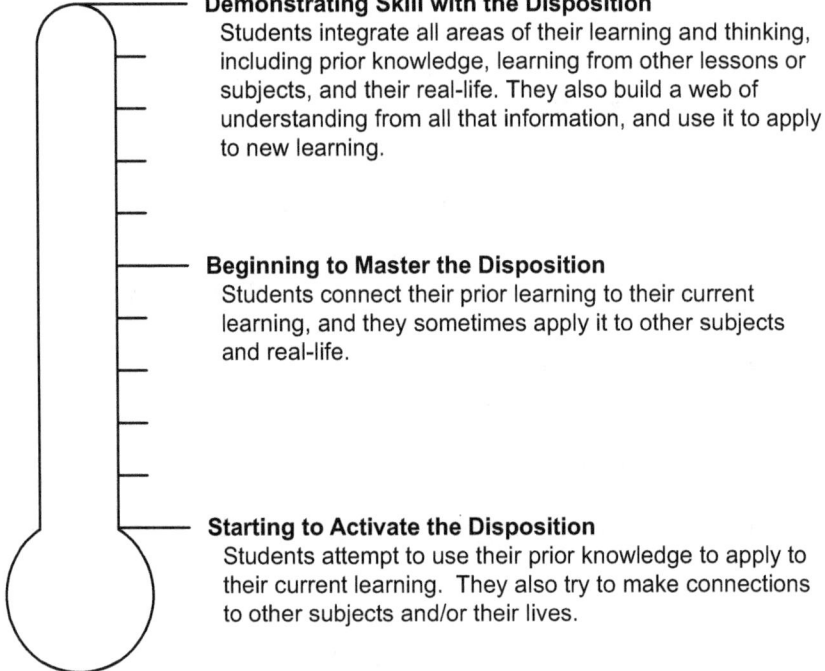

Demonstrating Skill with the Disposition
Students integrate all areas of their learning and thinking, including prior knowledge, learning from other lessons or subjects, and their real-life. They also build a web of understanding from all that information, and use it to apply to new learning.

Beginning to Master the Disposition
Students connect their prior learning to their current learning, and they sometimes apply it to other subjects and real-life.

Starting to Activate the Disposition
Students attempt to use their prior knowledge to apply to their current learning. They also try to make connections to other subjects and/or their lives.

Making Connections Activity

Grade One

Students read a book about "My Neighborhood." Then, using a Venn Diagram, they connect the neighborhood in the book with their own neighborhood.

Grade Four

Brainstorm a list of classroom and school rules. Then, read a book about colonial rules, such as the Mayflower Compact. Make connections between classroom rules, school rules, colonial rules, and any rules in your own life.

A Final Note

Student motivation impacts productive struggle, either positively or negatively, so we need to consider a student's motivation. We can temporarily impact extrinsic motivation or build a classroom environment that supports intrinsic motivation. Additionally, we need to foster five dispositions: Curiosity and Creative Thinking, Persistence and Self-Discipline, Strategic Problem-Solving and Metacognition, Risk-Taking, and Integrating Thinking.

Points to Ponder

1. How do you use extrinsic motivation in your classroom? How might you adjust your approach?
2. How can you incorporate aspects of intrinsic motivation in your classroom?
3. Which of the five dispositions would you like to focus on in your classroom?

Continue the Learning

Use the QR Code to access videos for your own use or for group professional development.

3

Instruction for Productive Struggle

The biggest question I hear about productive struggle is, "What does it look like in the classroom?" That's the question I will try to answer in this chapter. We'll start by looking at general principles for teaching productive struggle, then turn our attention to the "before-during-after process" of productive struggle, then finish with the teacher and student behaviors you see during the productive struggle process.

General Strategies for Teaching Productive Struggle

Let's start with discussing four general strategies to use when teaching productive struggle.

> Build a Climate for Productive Struggle
> Show Students What Good Looks Like
> Practice with a Partner (or Group)
> Independent Practice

Build a Climate for Productive Struggle

The first step in creating a productive struggle classroom is building a climate that will support that struggle. There are five aspects of a climate for productive struggle.

> Encourage Growth Mindset Behaviors
> Praise Risk-Taking

> Applaud Collaborative Work
> Celebrate Mistakes and Redirections
> Commend Perseverance and Resilience

Encourage Growth Mindset Behaviors

Do your students demonstrate growth mindset behaviors? They will need those to be successful. As we discussed in Chapter 2, there are specific student beliefs and behaviors that are essential for productive struggle. These are the ones you want to teach, facilitate, and encourage in your classroom.

> Focuses on continuous learning
> Learns from mistakes
> Believes in the power of effort
> Embraces challenge

Praise Risk-Taking

Next, it's important to praise and positively reinforce those times when students take risks. This might include when a student tentatively raises his hand, or when one of your students agrees to show her work to the class, or when someone takes the lead in a group activity. For students, each of these is a risk. So is attempting a task during productive struggle. Because the task is challenging, each of your students is risking that they might fail. So it's important to praise any attempts to take a risk. Let's look at sample praise statements.

> It's great that you chose to share your answer, even though you weren't sure you were correct.
>
> I admire how you took the lead in our group activity.
>
> Way to go! I'm so proud of you for raising your hand.
>
> You showed outstanding effort, really focusing on how to solve the problem.

Applaud Collaborative Work

Another characteristic you want to build as a part of your climate is the role of collaborative work. Students working together, learning together, supporting and encouraging each other is critical to successful productive struggle. There are three steps to building collaborative work in your classroom: modeling collaboration, providing structured, guided practice, and reinforcing positive efforts. In other words, teach collaboration just like you would teach any other skill.

Collaborative Learning

	You're a Team Player 3	You're Working on It . . . 2	You're the Lone Ranger 1	Total for Each Category
G Group Dedication	I listened respectfully to my teammates' ideas and offered suggestions that helped my group.	I did listen to ideas, but I didn't give suggestions.	I was distracted and more interested in the other groups than my group.	**Group Dedication** I circled number 3 2 1
R Responsibility	I eagerly accepted responsibility with my group and tried to do my part to help everyone in my group.	I accepted responsibility within my group without arguing.	I quarreled and did not accept roles given by my group.	**Responsibility** I circled number 3 2 1
O Open Communication	I listened to others' ideas and tried to solve conflicts peacefully.	I listened to others' ideas, but did not try to solve conflicts.	I was controlling and argumentative to my group.	**Open Communication** I circled number 3 2 1

(Continued)

Collaborative Learning

	You're a Team Player 3	You're Working on It . . . 2	You're the Lone Ranger 1	Total for Each Category
U Use of Work Time	I was involved and engaged; I encouraged my group the entire time we were working.	I tried my best the entire time we were working.	I was not involved and did not offer any suggestions for the good of the group.	**Use of Work Time** I circled number 3 2 1
P Participation	I was a team member. I offered ideas, suggestions, and help for my group.	I participated in the project, but did not offer to help anyone.	I did not participate because I was not interested.	**Participation** I circled number 3 2 1
				Total

Celebrate Mistakes and Redirections

Mistakes are a normal part of a productive struggle classroom. How we handle mistakes and the students who make them matters. I was in a classroom where a student had made a minor spelling mistake in her writing. The teacher scanned the writing, criticized the spelling, and moved on to the next student. The young girl was devastated, and from that point, she was a reluctant writer. The teacher didn't understand why the student didn't try anymore, but it was due to her negative reinforcement. A better approach would have been to use a praise sandwich: praise the content, ask questions about the spelling so the student could identify and redo the mistake, and praise her overall work.

An even better approach is a Marvelous Mistakes section on your wall. A teacher in Arizona shared this with me. Anytime a student makes a mistake, provide guidance so students can correct their own mistakes. Then, post both the mistake and the correction on the wall and have everyone cheer a Marvelous Mistake.

Commend Perseverance and Resilience

Finally, focus on the times when students persevere or show resilience. As with most of the other culture elements, if you commend students on their perseverance and resilience, they will try continue those efforts. What we reinforce, we will see again. If we repeat our praise, they will repeat their positive actions.

Student Behaviors	
Commend This . . .	*Not This . . .*
Student Puts Forth Effort	Student Gives Up Before He/She Starts
Student Tries Alternatives When Something Doesn't Work	Student Stops When Something Doesn't Work
Student Learns from Mistakes	Student Gets Stuck After a Mistake
After a Bad Grade, Student Reflects on What Happened so He/She Can Learn	After a Bad Grade, Student Gives Up

Show Students What Good Looks Like

It's critical to use the gradual release model to help students succeed with productive struggle. Begin by modeling what "good" productive struggle looks like. You'll also want to think aloud during the entire process to help students understand what is happening. When I was a beginning teacher, I modeled instructional processes, but just assumed my students knew what I was thinking. I quickly learned that wasn't true. As Patrice told me one day, "I see what you are doing, but I don't know why you are doing it." That's why it's so important to share your thinking.

> Okay, let's read this problem carefully. It says: "A baker made 156 cookies. She wants to pack them equally into boxes, with 12 cookies in each box. How many boxes will she need?" Hmm . . . I'm not sure of the answer right away, and that's okay. I'm going to think through it step by step.
>
> First, I'll restate the problem in my own words: There are 156 cookies, and I need to figure out how many groups of 12 will fit. That means I'm dividing 156 by 12. But division with big numbers can be tricky, so I'll try to break it apart.
>
> Let me think . . . 12 goes into 100 about 8 times because $8 \times 12 = 96$. Okay, I'll subtract 96 from 156. That leaves me with 60 cookies. But that's not enough. Should I start over and try to do a bigger number or should I work with the leftover number. Maybe that's easier.
>
> Now, how many times can 12 go into 60? Well, $5 \times 12 = 60$. Oh! So I can fit 5 more groups. It made more sense to do it that way since it was a smaller number.
>
> Now I'll add the groups together: 8 groups plus 5 groups equals 13 boxes total. Now, I need to double check my work and see if my answer makes sense, and I can do that with multiplication. $13 \times 12 = 156$. So, I am right!
>
> Whew—that took a bit of thinking and I wasn't sure at first, but I broke the problem into smaller parts, checked my work, and found the answer. That's productive struggle—I had to wrestle with it a little before I figured it out.

Notice how, in this productive struggle scenario, you are modeling everything the students can do. You showed the importance of restating the problem, chunking information, and double-checking their work with another strategy. You also showed that uncertainty is acceptable. Students will likely still struggle but preparing them ensures the struggle is productive.

Practice With a Partner or Group

After ensuring that students understand what you have modeled, move to a partner or group task. Either is acceptable; it just depends on your students. I sometimes prefer to use partners because it is a bit more manageable, but groups of 3 or 4 also work. Let's assume we are going to do a writing task with partners. You'll begin by introducing the task, reminding them of some scaffolding strategies (Chapter 5) that may be helpful, and then providing the productive struggle task.

> Provide students a story with an incomplete ending. Their task is to develop at least two possible endings, then choose the best option. They will also need to justify (either orally or in writing) why the one they chose is best, using evidence from the story.

As you are monitoring your pairs or groups, there are several key things you may observe. I've provided some possibilities, as well as the appropriate response.

What You Observe	
What You Observe	*What You Can Do*
Students can't seem to get started.	Ask questions that help them focus on the task and the concrete actions to take.
Students are stuck choosing the best option.	Remind them to think about what they know about story elements. How can that help them choose an option?
Students are struggling to justify their choice.	Ask students if they remember how to justify an answer. How have they done it in the past?

Notice the suggestions are all facilitative. You are not solving a problem for them; you are asking them questions or guiding them to think about something that might help them complete the task. It's tempting to want to provide too much help—resist that temptation! Remember, productive struggle means there should be some struggle.

Independent Practice

Finally, you want to give students the opportunity to practice on their own. Do not move to this step until students have been somewhat successful with a partner or a group. Also, part of gradual release is determining when to move to each step of the process. We'll be discussing choosing the right level of task in Chapter 4, but here, let me make one point. If this step is the first time students are working on their own, choose something that is challenging, but not necessarily highly challenging. The purpose here is *practice*. They are learning how to do this. Before they try productive struggle individually, discuss how they might handle different aspects of the struggle. I like to use an anchor chart with questions and discuss with the class possible answers.

Anchor Chart for Students	
What if I don't know how to get started?	
What if I get stuck?	
How do I know I'm on the right track?	
How do I know if I am successful?	

Perhaps this is your next task:

> Students will analyze two primary source documents about the same historical event and analyze how the authors' perspectives differ. Students should justify the elements of their analysis with specific evidence from the text, as well as other information from their own research and our class lessons.

Provide the productive struggle prompt to students and ask them to brainstorm with a partner the answer to the questions on the anchor chart. Then, discuss possible strategies with the whole group. You might see answers similar to those on the next page.

Anchor Chart for Primary Source Documents	
What if I don't know how to get started?	Read the documents. Write a summary of each document.
What if I get stuck?	Re-read the question to see what to do. Make a checklist of what to do. Use a graphic organizer to help with information.
How do I know I'm on the right track?	Am I following the task? I might turn the task into a question and see if I can answer yes.
How do I know if I am successful?	Did I address all parts of the question or task? Can I ask someone else in the class to check my work?

As you look at the sample questions and student responses, you'll notice that students are still struggling through the process; they just discuss possible ways they can address the struggle.

Do This . . . Not That With Students

Dr. Katie Perez, elementary curriculum specialist and former teacher from New Braunfels, Texas, recommends working with students to identify what is and is not productive. I like the headings she uses, asking students to discuss what parts of productive struggle should and should not feel and look like.

Productive Struggle
- Working through challenges to lead to Learning and growth!

When?	Should NOT feel/look like ✗	What it should feel/look like ✓
I'm Stuck	• give up/frustrated • look at someone else's work/cheating • asking for the answer • "spinning our wheels" – working hard but getting nowhere • throw a fit • don't blame others	• take a break and come back or skip • use my tools/resources – anchor chart, PV disc, teacher • try another way (a new strategy) • what worked last time? • asking a friend for help not the answer • ask questions? • breath
Working with partners/group	• arguing over the jobs/solution • one person does all the work/thinking • distracting others • one person taking over • only trying one way/one idea • saying "told you so" • don't play	• talk about the solutions • work with other people sometimes • take turns • share ideas and don't interrupt others • try a different way/strategy • value other people's ideas • listening to others • respectful

Before-During-After Productive Struggle

Too often, we think of productive struggle as an isolated event rather than a part of the overall instructional process. Simply throwing students into productive struggle isn't productive—it's just struggle. Let's look at what happens before, during, and after productive struggle.

Before Productive Struggle

Before students engage in productive struggle, there are key actions we need to take as teachers.

> ***Before Productive Struggle***
> Pre-Assessment
> Consideration of Prior Knowledge/Readiness
> Planning

First, we'll need some type of pre-assessment to help us ensure that the productive struggle is effective. You might use information from a previous lesson, a short pre-test, or anticipation guide to help you gather data.

Directions: Before we read, mark whether you agree or not with the statement, choosing a smile or a frown. After we read, we'll go back and check your answers. Be ready to explain what you learned!

Statement	Before Reading (T/F)	After Reading (T/F)
1.	☺ ☹	☺ ☹
2.	☺ ☹	☺ ☹
3.	☺ ☹	☺ ☹
4.	☺ ☹	☺ ☹

Sometimes connected to the pre-assessment is the consideration of students' prior knowledge and readiness. We may have this information from previous work or assessments with students, or we may want to do a separate activity to help prepare students for the productive struggle. Many teachers use a K-W-L before a lesson, which you'll see in Chapter 6.

Then, you'll use all this information to plan your instruction. Whenever you plan, take into consideration the following aspects.

Aspects to Consider

How this lesson fits into your overall scope and sequence.

How the productive struggle activity fits into the lesson.

How the productive struggle activity addresses your standard/goal/objective.

Whether students are prepared with the needed dispositions for the activity (Chapter 2).

Whether students are prepared with any needed prerequisite knowledge.

How students are prepared for self-scaffolding (Chapter 5) if needed.

How the productive struggle activity will be structured for students.

How you will structure groups if this is a partner or group task (Chapter 5).

During Productive Struggle

Productive struggle becomes a part of your lesson. Let's look at 3 activities that occur during productive struggle.

During Productive Struggle

Instruction/Scaffolding

Ongoing Assessment

Adjustments

First, you have your instruction, which includes scaffolding. Your planning, which was based on what you know about your students, will provide the framework for how productive struggle fits into the overall flow of the lesson. For example, you may need to incorporate an introductory activity before productive struggle, or, based on prior lessons, you may jump right into the productive struggle task. You also may need to pre-teach particular scaffolding and metacognitive strategies. There's not a perfect time; it depends on your students' readiness.

Then, you will have the productive struggle activity itself. Sometimes we fall into linear thinking—this will happen first, this second, this third. Productive struggle is a bit more amorphous. You may set up a sequence, but the very nature of struggle means it won't necessarily go in a straight line. Different students will hit stumbling blocks and use strategies you have taught them to self-correct and move forward; others may need you to provide some guided questioning (Chapter 6). Most importantly, you may not be able to predict what will happen. With planning, you'll set up a task designed to allow them to struggle (Chapter 4), but some will react in unexpected ways. Be prepared to provide appropriate guidance, always with an eye toward student independence.

Next, you will use ongoing formative assessment (Chapter 7) to see where students are and where they are going. Formative assessment can help you identify strengths and weaknesses, and particularly help you see where you need to make adjustments. That's the third part of productive struggle, making adjustments in order to have a more productive and successful experience.

Let's look at how this might play out in the classroom.

In this elementary science example, the teacher needed to make adjustments to the level of the task, as the original task was too simplistic.

Sample Productive Struggle Lesson Description (Elementary Science)

In a lesson on shadows and lights, students are asked to make shadows change using flashlights and different objects. Midway through the activity, it becomes clear to the teacher that this is actually too easy for students. She poses another question to the class: How can you make shadows where the shadow is always bigger than the object? Students immediately engaged, trying different ways to make the shadows bigger, rather than the same size. Once they mastered this, she posed another question, " How can you make shadows where the shadow is the same size as the object? How can you make a smaller shadow?" Building on the larger shadows, students struggled to make both smaller and same-size shadows, but were able to accomplish the tasks.

After Productive Struggle

> ### *After Productive Struggle*
> Summative Assessment
> Reflection
> Short- and Long-Term Planning

Finally, after students have completed the productive struggle activity, there are three actions for you to take. First, provide some form of summative assessment to determine what students have learned. You may decide to assess only content, or you may want to assess the productive struggle process (Chapter 6). Either is fine.

Next, you'll reflect on what you learned from the formative assessments during the lesson and the summative assessment. Did students master or show progress toward a particular objective or skill? Did they truly struggle or was the task too easy? Or, was the struggle frustrating—the task was too hard or they were unprepared?

With the chart below, you log each objective and note the percentage of your students who mastered the objective, are progressing toward the objective, or have not mastered the objective.

Content Knowledge Reflection			
Objective	*Mastered*	*Progressing*	*Not Mastered*

With the process of productive struggle, you might note broader information. You can use this as a check-off, or you can designate how many/what percentage of your students fit in each category.

Productive Struggle Process Reflection			
Task	Just Right	Too Hard	Too Easy

Needed Adjustments		
Skill	Yes	No
Students Had Appropriate Prior Knowledge		
Students Were Prepared with Self-Monitoring Skills		
Students Made Adjustments as Needed		
Students Used Scaffolding Skills		

Finally, use your reflections to plan for the future—both short term and long term. What needs to happen immediately? What do you need to do to help students be prepared in the future? Be sure to log this information so you will have it for additional planning and instruction.

Additional Reflective Notes	
Based on . . .	I Need to . . .
Content Knowledge Mastery	
Students' Skills During Productive Struggle	
The Amount of Struggle	
The Effectiveness of Struggle	
My Other Observations	

Teacher Behaviors for Productive Struggle

Now that we've looked at before, during, and after instruction, let's turn our attention to teacher behaviors. There are specific teacher behaviors that support productive struggle. As I detailed in Chapter 1, these are based on John Hattie's effect sizes. Let's look at six.

> *Teacher Behaviors*
>
> Teacher Expectations
> Goals and Criteria
> Consideration of Prior Knowledge and Ability
> Teacher Clarity and Interpretations
> Classroom Methods and Strategies
> Scaffolding for Learning

Teacher Expectations

Teachers' beliefs, reflected in actions, demonstrate their expectations for their students. In other words, teachers treat students differently dependent on "expectancy," or what they expect. Although the difference in treatment may not be intentional, students notice it and will meet those expectations no matter how high or low they are (Williamson & Blackburn, 2016).

How do our behaviors reflect our expectations? For example, teachers tend to probe students more if they have high expectations. This sends a clear message that "I know you know the answer, and if I give you hints, you will formulate a reasonable response." Teachers also demonstrate expectations in the types of assignments or activities implemented in the classroom. Abbigail Armstrong remembered a time when her gifted students participated in thought-provoking activities such as figuring out the rise of a ramp to meet regulation to be fitted on a building, whereas her "general classes" were given drill-and-practice assignments with very little discussion of solutions and perspectives. As described by Robert Marzano (2010), let's look at typical behaviors related to low and high expectations of students.

Differential Treatment of High- and Low-Expectancy Students

	Affective Tone	*Academic Content Interactions*
Negative	Less eye contact Smile less Less physical contact	Call on less often Provide less wait time Ask less challenging questions
	More distance from student's seat Engage in less playful or light dialogue Use of comfort talk (That's okay, you can be good at other things) Display angry disposition	Ask less specific questions Delve into answers less deeply Reward them for less challenging responses Provide answers for students Use simpler modes of presentation and evaluation Do not insist that homework be turned in on times Use comments such as, "Wow, I'm surprised you answered correctly" Use less praise
Positive	More eye contact Smile more More physical contact Less distance from student's seat Engage in more playful or light dialogue Little use of comfort talk (That's okay, you can be good at other things)	Call on more often Provide more wait time Ask more challenging questions Ask more specific questions Delve into answers more deeply Reward them for more challenging responses Use more complex modes of presentation and evaluation Insist that homework be turned in on time Use more praise

Marzano also provides a four-step process for identifying and addressing these differences in expectations. I've added suggestions for each step, which are helpful as you consider how to ensure overall high expectations for your students.

Marzano's Four-Step Process to Identifying Expectation Behaviors
Step 1: Identify students for whom you have low expectations.
Create a three-column chart and label each column High Expectations, Low Expectations, No Expectations. This may be a difficult task, so think of it in terms of when it comes to completing an assignment, who will turn it in early, who will turn it in on the due date with minutes to spare and who will not even bother.
Step 2: Identify similarities in students.
Consider ways your students are similar. Ask yourself, "Do I have similar expectations because of my students' similarities?" "Are my expectations high or low?" The similarities may be skin color, ethnicity, cultural group, sex or gender. This, too, is not an easy task. Discovering our own biases is challenging but if you confront why you are treating your students differently, you can begin your journey to equity in expectations.
Step 3: Identify differential treatment of low-expectancy and high-expectancy students (see previous chart).
Step 4: Treat low-expectancy and high-expectancy students the same.
Choose three behaviors that you discovered you use with students for whom you have high expectations and practice these behaviors for a few days. It may be that you choose to smile at all students. It may be that if any student gives you an incorrect answer, you will give the student process time or time to ask a friend before moving on. Whatever the behavior, keep a log of the behavior and who received the treatment. Also consider technology and apps that can facilitate the change. For example, Random by ClassDojo, Transum Name Selecting App, and Random Student Selector by LiveSchool allow you to call on random students to ensure that you do not limit your choice of students for responses.

Teacher behaviors are also evidenced in the instructional tasks and assignments we ask students to complete. We'll delve into this aspect in Chapter 4, but for now, let's look at a variety of elementary school tasks that reflect teacher behaviors.

Kindergarten

> Provide sample materials such as paper, tape, and straws and ask them to make something that can stand tall without falling over.

In this task, students are asked to provide a solution to something that is unpredictable, which provides a level of challenge. It also doesn't have one correct answer.

Grade One

> Ask students to write directions for something they do regularly (like make a peanut butter and jelly sandwich). Then, see if a partner can follow the directions and complete the task correctly.

This is a challenging task, because most students will not provide a clear, thorough, correct set of directions. They may skip steps or just assume their partner will know what to do. The challenge becomes to rewrite them after their partner tries to complete the task.

Grade Two

> Students choose two colors of crayons. Then, ask them to create a scene from nature.

Because students only have two colors, they'll need to use critical thinking about blending, shading, and problem-solving with limitations.

Grade Three

> After reading several fables, ask students to write their own fable, which must include a lesson to be learned.

In addition to applying what they know about fables, students must create their own fable that teaches a lesson. Tying the fable to a specific lesson provides a level of challenge.

Grade Four

> Read two primary sources about a historical event that describe the event differently. Students must determine how and why they are different.

Another great open-ended activity, students will likely struggle to identify why the two sources are different. Understanding biases and different perspectives is an excellent activity.

Grade Five

> Review the three math problems, each of which represent a real-life situation, as well as their solutions. Determine which, if any, of the solved problems are incorrect. If there is an equation that is solved incorrectly, justify why it is incorrect, solve it correctly, and explain how you know it is now correct.

There are several characteristics of a challenging assignment reflected earlier. First, students are required to recognize and explain misconceptions, which is an aspect of reasoning as they consider the appropriateness of the solutions to the problems. Next, they must verify the reasonableness of their answers and provide a sound argument in support of their response that elaborates on the real-life situations.

Goals and Criteria

As you plan your lessons, it's important to have clear learning goals and criteria that are appropriately challenging (Chapter 4). One strategy I like is the concept of SMART goals.

> **SMART**
> S   Specific
> M   Measurable
> A   Attainable
> R   Realistic
> T   Timely

One mistake I often see is that teachers use standards or objectives from another source. For example, I saw the following objective: Students will realize how living things adapt to their environment. What does it mean to realize something? How will students demonstrate understanding? Do they already know information about living things? Here's a SMART version of the same objective.

> By the end of the unit, students will be able to identify at least three specific ways that animals adapt survive in their environment and accurately explain how each adaptation supports survival, as measured by a writing assessment with 80% accuracy.

Additionally, students must understand the criteria for success. You'll want to plan for this from the start of your planning. Do you want them to be able to answer a specific question? Do you want them to write an essay with three key points and evidence for each point? Be sure they know how they should show what they know. I've found rubrics are particularly helpful—they help me clarify what I'm looking for and they help students understand what I think "good looks like."

Community Workers Assignment Rubric (Grades 2–3)		
Assessment Criteria	*Strong*	*Developing*
Information about Community Worker	Clearly explains who the worker is, what they do, and why they are important with good details	Gives a basic explanation with some details missing
Examples	Includes clear examples (tools, uniforms, places they work, how they help)	Includes a few examples, but may be incomplete

Community Workers Assignment Rubric (Grades 2–3)		
Assessment Criteria	Strong	Developing
Organization and Clarity	Information is well organized and easy to understand	Information is somewhat organized but may be hard to follow
Creativity/Effort	Work shows strong effort and creativity (color, neatness, extra details)	Work shows some effort and creativity

Consideration of Prior Knowledge and Ability

Third, teachers who encourage productive struggle consider prior knowledge and ability when planning lessons. Yes, you want to provide challenging tasks, but you don't want to ignore your students' readiness to learn. We'll look at multiple ways to assess prior knowledge in Chapter 5 (Scaffolding), but here let's look readiness.

Readiness

The heart of teaching is to take a student from where he or she is, and move him or her to a higher level of learning. To do that, you need to understand where a student is in terms of knowledge and understanding. Ideally, you assess readiness levels before you start units or lessons, and you continue to assess changing readiness levels using formative assessments.

Pre-Tests

I've known teachers who use a pre-test for the year, using a broad range of questions to identify topics that might need less instruction. A far more effective approach in my experience, is to use pre-testing to measure students' understanding of key topics, which usually means a learning unit, such as a two-week study of landforms.

> **Characteristics of Effective Pre-Tests**
> Focused on essential skills
> Incorporates questions that determine if they understand necessary background knowledge

> Incorporates questions that determine if they understand concepts planned for instruction
>
> Incorporates questions that determine if they have advanced knowledge of concepts
>
> Is not overwhelming for students
>
> Questions are clear and understandable

Observations

An important formative assessment tool for teachers is the use of observations. Observations can be planned, or they can be spontaneous. In an observation, you simply observe what students are doing, and take notes for documentation. You may choose to observe for particular instructional behaviors, or you may simply observe to see what happens from a general standpoint. Checklists, which provide a quick way for you to make notes about your observations can be simple yes/no tallies, or they can be open-ended for teachers to add notes.

Sample Writing Checklist

> ____Student writes about the topic.
>
> ____Student writes a beginning, middle, and end.
>
> ____Student gives examples for statements.

Interviews and Conferences

In interviews and conferences, the teacher meets with students to assess understanding of content. For either of these, the teacher plans a series of questions to ask a student about his or her learning. It's also important to stay flexible and adjust questions during the interview or conference. These are probably used most often in writing situations, but they can be used with any subject area.

Sample Writing Conference Questions

> Please tell me a little about your writing.
>
> What do you think is going well?
>
> Show me an example of that.

> What are you struggling with?
> Show me an example.
> How do you think you can improve on your own?
> How can I help you?
> What are your next steps?

Teacher Clarity and Interpretations

Another evidence-based key to effective instruction, especially in the productive struggle classroom, is related to teacher clarity and interpretations. There are three aspects in this area.

> Teacher clarity.
> Organization of instruction.
> Interpretations based on assessment of student learning.

As we consider clarity, I remember a situation when I was a teacher. I had explained something to my students, but they didn't understand. I explained again, but they were still confused. One of my students said, "Can you just tell us what's in your head?" That clicked with me. I just assumed they knew certain concepts, but they didn't. I decided to "think like a beginner" and taught the lesson again, this time successfully. When I clarified my instruction, the students were successful.

Also, your instruction should be organized in a way to maximize learning. This includes activating prior knowledge, connecting to other learning, and providing options for applying learning to real life. You can also use the 5E method, which was developed by Roger Bybee and his colleagues.

> Engage
> Explore
> Explain
> Elaborate
> Evaluate

A final aspect of this category is that effective teachers make interpretations based on assessment of student learning. In other words, as you incorporate formative assessment throughout your lesson, you actually use that information to make instructional adjustments. We'll talk more about this in Chapter 6.

Classroom Methods and Strategies

There are a variety of classroom strategies and methods that are particularly effective in the productive struggle classroom. Although we won't go into detail on each at this time, notice that in all of the options listed later, there is a high level of student involvement and student ownership, and a shift in the teacher's role to facilitator.

> Small Group
> Class Discussion
> Inquiry-Based Teaching
> Constructivist Teaching
> Inductive Teaching
> Cognitive Task Analysis
> Problem-Solving Teaching
> Teaching Students to Drive Their Learning
> Self-regulation Learning

Scaffolding for Learning

Finally, teachers who encourage productive struggle provide scaffolding, including giving examples and offering guided practice. Chapter 5 focuses specifically on these incorporating these areas, but for now, let's look at a rubric overview.

Rubric for Teacher Behaviors			
	Beginning	*Emerging*	*Accomplished*
Teacher Expectations	Expectations are based on preconceived and perhaps outdated notions of what students should be able to do. Expectations differ based on the identified label of each student (special needs, honors, etc.).	Expectations are built on what students are currently able to do, with some ideas about raising the level of challenge. There is an acknowledgement that teachers play a role in helping students meet high expectations. There are also high expectations for advanced and/or gifted students.	Expectations are balanced between what students can currently do, but what they have the potential to do. High expectations incorporate that part of the teacher's role is to scaffold students for success.
Goals and Criteria	Goals are general; criteria is somewhat clear.	Goals are specific, with general criteria for students.	SMART goals provide very clear criteria for success.
Consideration of Prior Knowledge and Ability	There is minimal understanding of students' prior knowledges and abilities based on existing information. The understanding is minimally reflected in lesson planning and implementation.	There is some understanding of students' prior knowledges and abilities based on some assessments. The understanding is reflected in lesson planning and implementation.	A detailed understanding of prior knowledge and ability is built on multiple sources and is thoroughly integrated into lesson planning and implementation.

(Continued)

Rubric for Teacher Behaviors

	Beginning	*Emerging*	*Accomplished*
Teacher Clarity and Interpretations	Teacher provides lessons that are sometimes clear and detailed, somewhat organized, and may or may not reflect interpretations of assessment of student learning.	Teacher provides lessons that are clear, somewhat detailed, organized, and somewhat reflect interpretations of assessment of student learning.	Teacher provides lessons that are clear, detailed, extremely organized, and thoroughly reflect interpretations of assessment of student learning.
Classroom Strategies and Methods	Teacher either minimally uses or does not use evidence-based strategies and methods that are conducive to productive struggle.	Teacher uses some evidence-based strategies and methods that are conducive to productive struggle.	Teacher incorporates evidence-based strategies and methods that are conducive to productive struggle.
Scaffolding for Learning	Teacher uses scaffolding, generally for all students that supports the productive struggle classroom.	Teacher sometimes incorporates scaffolding for all students that supports the productive struggle classroom. He or she attempts to individual scaffolding.	Teacher thoroughly incorporates scaffolding, both general and individualized, that supports the productive struggle classroom.

Student Behaviors

Now let's turn our attention from teacher behaviors to student behaviors, such as students' self-expectations, self-regulation, metacognitive reflection, and learning together.

Expectations

Just as teachers' expectations matter, so do students' expectations. A student's expectations of himself or herself drive much of what happens with learning. How can we help build students' expectations? We discussed this in Chapter 2, but as a brief recap, here are some strategies.

> Believe each student has unlimited potential.
> Encourage them whenever they make a mistake.
> Support students to ensure growth.
> Create a growth mindset.
> Challenge them in learning activities.

Self-regulation

Self-regulation for students involves several areas: effort, concentration, persistence, and engagement.

We want students to show effort and persistence because it positively impacts student learning. Encouraging and reinforcing effort are particularly critical for those students who do not understand the importance of their own efforts. In *Classroom Instruction that Works*, Marzano, Pickering, and Pollock (2001) make two important comments regarding students' views about effort.

> ### *Research-Based Generalizations About Effort*
> ♦ Not all students realize the importance of believing in effort.
> ♦ Students can learn to change their beliefs to an emphasis on effort.
> (Marzano et al., 2001, p. 50)

This is positive news for teachers. First, we're not imagining it—students don't realize they need to exert effort. And second, we can help them change that belief. Richard Curwin describes seven specific ways to encourage effort.

---

7 Ways to Encourage Effort

1. Never fail a student who tries, and never give the highest grades to one who doesn't.
2. Start with the positive.
3. See mistakes as learning opportunities, not failures.
4. Give do overs.
5. Give students the test before you start a unit.
6. Limit your corrections.
7. Do not compare students.

We also want students to show concentration and engagement. When they are involved in learning, they typically concentrate of the activity, becoming highly engaged. This happens when they are intrinsically motivated (Chapter 2), and when we create opportunities for them to be engaged. Productive struggle is an ideal activity for concentration and engagement, especially if designed well. We'll look more at this in Chapter 4, where we explore how to pick the right tasks and activities.

Metacognitive Reflection

Another key for your students is their metacognitive reflection. There are five types of metacognitive reflection.

Evaluation and reflection
Strategy monitoring
Self-judgement and reflection
Metacognitive strategies
Self-verbalization and self-questioning

Students don't learn these strategies on their own; we need to model them, teach them, and allow them to practice them. We'll look at how to do that in Chapter 5 (Scaffolding).

Learning Together

Students in a productive struggle classroom also learn together. Even when they are working individually, they reach out to each other for feedback. There are five ways students learn together.

> Questioning
> Elaborative interrogation
> Collaborative learning
> Reciprocal teaching
> Classroom discussion

There are specific strategies that support each of these five options. We'll discuss them in Chapter 5.

> ### *Self-Scaffolding Strategies*
> Organizing and transforming notes
> Study skills
> Concept mapping
> Graphic organizers and concept maps
> Elaboration and organization

Now, let's look at a rubric to assess student behaviors.

	Rubric for Student Behaviors		
	Beginning	*Emerging*	*Accomplished*
Student Expectations	Teacher attempts to model high expectations for students, believes that some students can learn at high levels, and tries to help some students develop a growth mindset. A few students have high expectations for themselves.	Teacher sometimes models high expectations for students, believes that some students can learn at high levels, and helps all students develop a growth mindset. This results in some students having high expectations for themselves.	Teacher models high expectations for students, believes that each student can learn at high levels, encourages and supports those high expectations, and helps all students develop a growth mindset. This results in all students having high expectations for themselves.
Self-Regulation	Some students demonstrate effort, concentration, persistence, and engagement, but the majority do not.	Students sometimes demonstrate effort, concentration, persistence, and engagement.	Students consistently demonstrate high levels of effort, concentration, persistence, and engagement.

Rubric for Student Behaviors			
	Beginning	*Emerging*	*Accomplished*
Metacognitive Reflection	Teacher may teach students a metacognitive strategy. Students may or may not use the strategy during productive struggle.	Teacher teaches students some metacognitive strategies and gives opportunities for practice. Students sometimes use metacognitive strategies during productive struggle.	Teacher teaches students a variety of strategies for metacognitive reflection, models their use, and gives opportunities for guided and independent practice. Students utilize the metacognitive strategies appropriately during productive struggle.
Learning Together	Teacher provides some activities for students to learn together. Students attempt to work together to complete a task.	Teacher provides a variety of structured activities for students to learn together. Students collaborate at some level to help each other learn.	Teacher provides a variety of well-designed, structured activities for students to learn together. Students collaborate at high levels to help each other learn.

(Continued)

Rubric for Student Behaviors			
	Beginning	*Emerging*	*Accomplished*
Self-Scaffolding Strategies	Teacher may teach students a self-scaffolding strategy. Students may or may not use the strategy during productive struggle.	Teacher teaches students some self-scaffolding strategies and gives opportunities for practice. Students sometimes use self-scaffolding strategies during productive struggle.	Teacher teaches students a variety of self-scaffolding strategies, models their use, and gives opportunities for guided and independent practice. Students utilize the self-scaffolding strategies appropriately during productive struggle.

A Final Note

To build a productive struggle classroom, teachers need to build a climate, and teach students how to successfully participate in productive struggle. Then, it's important to provide instruction that supports productive struggle before, during, and after the task. Finally, you'll want to incorporate the teacher and student behaviors that support productive instruction.

Points to Ponder

1. What can you do to improve your climate so it will support productive struggle?
2. Which of the before-during-after strategies do you want to try?
3. What teacher behaviors do you exhibit? Are there ways to improve?
4. What student behaviors would you like to encourage?

Continue the Learning

Use the QR Code to access videos for your own use or for group professional development.

4

What Is the Right Level for Productive Struggle?

One of the key concerns with productive struggle is how to determine the right level of the task or material. In other words, how do I know if something is too hard, too easy, or just right? In this chapter, we'll look at five areas that can help us make that determination.

> Vygotsky's Zone of Proximal Development
> Flow from Mihaly Csikszentmihalyi
> Determining Appropriately Leveled Text Materials
> Appropriately Challenging Skills and Tasks
> What Is the Difference Between An Explanation and a Justification?

Vygotsky's Zone of Proximal Development

In 1978, Lev Vygotsky theorized that there is a zone of proximal development (ZPD) for learners. He posits that students sometimes do work that is too easy or is in their comfort zone. Other times, they work at a level that is too challenging therefore, they are in a frustration level. In the zone of proximal development, students are working at the ideal learning level. Students may need help, or they may have to persist to be successful, but this is where they learn best.

He provides more detail:

> The distance between the actual developmental level (of the learner) as determined by independent problem solving and the level of potential development as determined through problem solving under adult guidance, or in collaboration with more capable peers.
> (Vygotsky, 1978, p. 86)

Let's review his words: we are looking at the distance between the actual developmental level and the potential developmental level. That's the area of potential growth, and it's exactly the sweet spot for productive struggle. Determining the ZPD comes from assessment, which we'll speak to in Chapter 6. However, he also notes that adult guidance or collaboration is needed. In other words, scaffolding, which we'll address in Chapter 5, is critical.

Critical Components of the Zone of Proximal Development

Assessment to Determine Current Developmental Level

Vision of Potential Developmental Level

Guidance and Collaboration

Scaffolding

These components provide key structural components for teachers to help meet students' needs.

Flow From Mihaly Csikszentmihalyi

In 1975, psychologist Mihaly Csiksentmihalyi introduced the concept of flow, which is a mental state that occurs when a person is completely immersed in a task or activity. There are several characteristics of flow.

Complete concentration

A full understanding of what to do

Intrinsic motivation

Appropriately challenging level of skill

As with Vygotsky's Zone of Proximal Development, students are working at a level that provides challenge—just not too much. Csikszentmihalyi describes that level as occurring when "one's skills are adequate to cope with the challenges at hand, in a goal-directed, rule-bound action system that provides clear clues as to how one is performing" (2009). For teachers, this implies that we need to equip students (Chapter 5) with skills, such as problem-solving, that allow them to meet the challenge, and that we need to provide structure (Chapter 3) to help them be successful.

Determining Appropriately Leveled Text Materials

Oftentimes, because we want student to be successful, we move them into materials that are in their comfort zone. One of the major areas for productive struggle is through the texts used during teaching. It's important for students to read a book or an article they can quickly and easily finish; those opportunities build self-confidence, provide enjoyable experiences, increase fluency and may increase student motivation. But if that's all students read, they never learn how to deal with more challenging materials. We should consider providing text materials in all subject areas that are in a student's zone of proximal development.

I'd like to take a moment and add a cautionary note to our discussion. The concept of leveled texts can be controversial, mainly because they have been misused at times. For example, I visited a school where every book was labeled with a number and students were never allowed to read a book that was not in their identified range. I spoke to a student who wanted to read a higher-level book, and he was very motivated by the topic. However, the teacher told him no because of the number. That's not best practice with leveling. A student who is highly motivated by the topic can often push through and read a more challenging book. Leveled text is a guide, not a limitation. Another example is with a struggling student who doesn't have much confidence in himself. In that case, I may want to help him choose an easier book to build fluency and confidence, in order to then move back up to something more challenging. And there are some books that may have a lower score on a readability scale, but the content is more difficult, perhaps due to the concepts described or the use of figurative language. Using leveled text is more of an art than a science, and it's critical that you use your judgment as a part of the process.

Now, what are the positive reasons to use leveled text? The authors of *Beyond Leveled Text* (2nd edition) describe seven aspects of leveling books for readers.

Readers make the most progress when books are not too easy or too difficult.

Considering a just-right level helps readers read fluently and comprehend better; thus they take of the traits and skills of better readers.

Students who meet success in reading are more likely to persist, to read more with less off-task behavior, and to achieve more.

Acceleration in learning, or increased achievement, is possible for struggling readers when the text/reading level is match.

> Groups of books into levels can make it easier to teachers, parents, and children to select books to read.
>
> Books that are used for instruction can be selected with emphasis on student needs at a certain point, but selections should be different for independent reading.
>
> With the variety of books available with leveling features, schools can adapt a greater number of their book collections to support their particular students.

Look for a balance: Material should be difficult enough that students are learning something new, but not so hard that they give up. If you like to play tennis, you'll improve if you play against someone who is better than you. But if you play against Venus and Serena Williams, you'll learn less because you are overwhelmed by their advanced skill level. A good guideline is that for text to be appropriately challenging for growth, students should be able to understand about 75% of what they read. That percentage means students understand the majority of the material, while learning something new. One option for increasing text difficulty is to identify where your students are reading and provide text materials that match their level of growth.

When I was teaching, I used books that were labeled on grade level, but in reality, they were much easier than what students were expected to read on the state test or in real-life materials. That is still true today, and that is why it is important to use a measure that is consistent across all texts. There are a variety of readability formulas, which provide standard for text difficulty you can use to select texts.

Popular Readability Formulas	
Fry	The most widely used of the readability formulas. The Fry is based on the assumption that the longer the sentence and the longer the word, the more difficult the passage.
Flesch-Kincaid	The Flesch-Kincaid is embedded in Microsoft Word programs and checks documents for the reading level of the passage.

Popular Readability Formulas	
Fountas and Pinnell Benchmark Assessment System	There are 26 levels in the Fountas and Pinnell System
The Lexile Framework	The Lexile Framework is a computerized formula that analyzes entire text selections by sentence length and word frequency. It allows you to link difficulty of text materials with standardized tests. The web site provides a searchable database of books, and many national and state tests also provide Lexile levels for students based on test scores.

No matter which tool you use to determine the difficulty of text materials, remember that text difficulty is only one factor to consider when selecting text for or with your students. Other considerations include the appropriateness of the text for the students' age or developmental levels, the content of the material, and the purpose for reading, such as for interest or research.

Considerations for Text Selection

Is the content of the text pertinent to my standards or objectives?

Is the content of the text appropriate to the purpose of the assignment (independent reading, research, partner reading, etc.)?

Is the content of the text appropriate to the age or developmental level of my students?

Is the content of the text appropriately challenging for growth (not too hard, yet not too easy)?

Is this the only opportunity my students will be given to read, or are they allowed choices at other times?

Remember to always use your professional judgment when selecting text materials for your struggling students. Any readability formula may be the starting point for book selection, but it should never be the only factor considered. The goal is always to pick the right resource for the right reader at the right time. Remember to think about all aspects of the book or text and preview materials to ensure they are appropriate for your students.

Students' Determination of Reading Level

You may have situations where you want students to self-determine if a book is appropriately challenging. Here's a simple three level rubric students can use to choose a leveled text. Note that my levels equate appropriately challenging with productive struggle—they are more challenging than some other rules in existence, such as the Goldilocks Rules.

Choose a book or article you would like to read. Read it to yourself and count the number of words you don't know or understand. Choose the column with the number of words.		
0-2 Words	3-6	7 or More
Very Easy	Appropriately Challenging	Too Hard

Ultimately, what you want to do is balance the level of materials for your students. Too often, we lower the level of text for our struggling students, especially in the content areas such as science and social studies. A part of high expectations is providing text that is challenging for students, then balancing that challenge by providing the appropriate support and scaffolding so students can be successful.

Appropriately Challenging Skills and Tasks

Finally, we'll turn our attention to appropriately challenging skills and tasks. How do we determine what is appropriately challenging? As we've discussed earlier in this chapter, you'll want to use your judgment in making final decisions, but I wanted to give you a guide that describes key skills and tasks that are challenging. This is built on national frameworks such as Depth of Knowledge and the Cognitive Rigor Matrix, as well as my extensive work for over 20 years on rigor. You may find that you need to start with the chart for Developing Skills, but I'd encourage you to move to the set of Appropriately Challenging Criteria. Your students may struggle, but that's the point!

There are many skills we assume are challenging to students, but they actually aren't. It's important to recognize that these skills may develop the skills needed for challenging work, but they aren't what we are looking at for productive struggle.

Developing Skills

Apply
Summarize
Interpret
Predict
Infer
Compare and contrast
Relevant/irrelevant information
Explaining
Locating information
Developing hypotheses
Select math procedure according to criteria
Create diagram or model to demonstrate understanding

I understand you may be thinking that, for some of your students, especially younger students, the developing tasks are challenging. When students haven't been working at challenging levels, then these tasks are difficult. But that shouldn't be the goal. Each of these tasks should be considered building blocks—something that is a stepping stone to truly challenging work. They may even be part of a student task, one that is a precursor for appropriately challenging work.

So what types of tasks and activities are considered challenging?

> **Appropriately Challenging Work for Productive Struggle**
>
> Identifying and explaining misconceptions (error analysis)
> Proposing and evaluating solutions
> Justifications, going beyond the text
> Defending with evidence
> Open-ended situations
> Synthesizing
> Generalizing
> Reframing ideas
> Grappling with complex text
> Identifying questions and designing investigations
> Designing mathematical models
> Analyzing how changes have affected people and places
> Developing alternate solutions
> Developing a logical argument for concepts

Let's look at sample productive struggle tasks, even for the youngest students, that reflect these appropriately challenging criteria. You'll notice how many are open ended, which provides an excellent opportunity for productive struggle.

Kindergarten

In this interactive game, small groups of students identify words that do and do not begin with a sound.

> Students take turns playing the Red Herring Game. Each group stands up, states a letter (A-Z), then shares three words. Other students identify the word that does not start with the stated letter.

In our second kindergarten activity, students think about problems they see in their classroom.

> Students design a rule to solve a classroom problem.

Grade One

Here's an example from Grade 1 that asks students to identify and explain misconceptions.

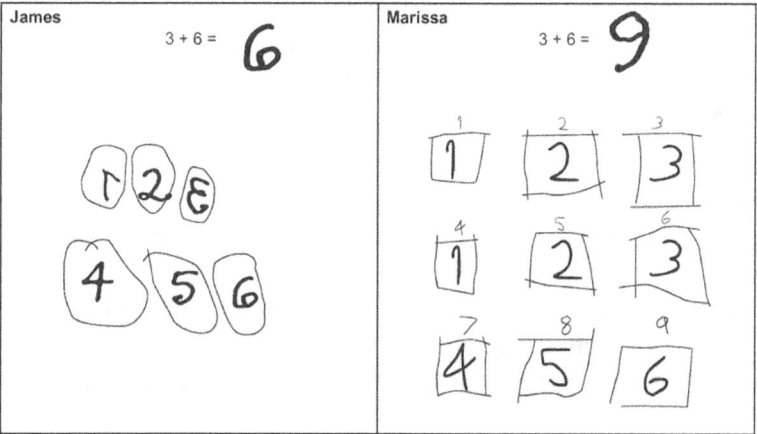

A first grade teacher builds on sequencing by adding justification to the task.

> The teacher provides pictures from a story. After sequencing the pictures, students explain how the scene changed over time. They also elaborate on their explanation by justifying the changes with specific examples from the story.

Primary Grades

Consider a primary grades reading example.

> We have just finished reading *The Frog Book*, which told us all about frogs. Today, we're going to read *The Frog Who Lost His Croak*. In addition to your regular questions, ask: How was the frog like the frogs in the first book? Was he like a real frog, or was he made up? Why do you think that? If The Frog Who Lost His Croak met the frogs in *The Frog Book*, what would he ask them? Why? What would the frogs in both books tell a baby frog are the most important things he or she should know in life?

Next, look at another reading example for primary grades.

> We have been reading and talking about the adventures of Tum Tum and Nutmeg. Living in a world where everything is considerably larger than them, we see their unique perspective on places and events that

are ordinary to us. Being "small" in your own world, how can you connect with these mice? Are there times when you wish you were bigger or older or that your voice was heard more clearly? Are there times when you "see" things differently than the adults around you? What would you say to the adults in your life about the way you see things?

Now let's read *Clifford, the Big Red Dog*. How is Clifford's view of the world very different than Emily Elizabeth's? What's different about seeing things from a much larger point of view? Imagine that you have been sent to a deserted island where everything is very, very small. Your view of the world would be quite different than the little people that live there. Using pictures and or/words, describe how you might see things from a different perspective. Create a video introducing yourself to the people who live there, explaining how you see things differently.

Grade Two

In a second grade social studies classroom, an application pushes students to analyze their own information and tie the information to a real-life job.

Students study community workers such as a police officer, firefighter, librarian, nurse, teacher, plumber, bus driver, or mayor. At the end of the unit, each student identifies a worker's job they would like, and they complete a job application.

Name_____ Date of Application _____

Which of the classroom jobs are you applying for? Write the job title on the line below.

_____

Why are you interested in this job?

_____

Analyze and describe how you are qualified for the job. You must include specific experiences you have had to prepare you and specific traits you have that qualify you. All examples must include why each prepares you for the job, linking to what you have learned about the job.

_____

_____

_____

This science example requires a high level of productive struggle, asking students to design an investigation, design a device, analyze data, and justify whether or not the design works.

Name: _____ Date: _____

Force and Motion

Obtain, evaluate, and communicate information to explain the effect of a force (a push or a pull) in the movement of an object (changes in speed or direction).

a. Plan and carry out an investigation to demonstrate how pushing and pulling on an object affects the motion of the object.

b. Design a device to change the speed or direction of an object.

c. Record and analyze data to decide if a design solution works as intended to change the speed or direction of an object with a force (a push or pull). Based on what you have learned in class, your data, and your life, why does your device do what I asked you to do?

Grade Three

With third graders, a comprehensive unit culminates in a project that asks students to design a school for Mars.

> As the culmination of a ten-day unit, students create a school on Mars to support the colonists' lives there. Students must figure out what the curriculum should be, the physical design of the school, and the design of the outside garden. It's important to note the curriculum needs to prepare students for jobs and real life on Mars. Specific reasons for each choice should be explained.

Next, students analyze math information, then recognize and explain misconceptions.

> Directions: Read each question two times. Please CIRCLE the correct answer for each question. Show your math thinking for each problem. It's okay to write on this test!
>
> $$3 \times 3 \times 3 > 9 \times 3$$
>
> a. False, because the product of 9 × 3 is greater than the product of 3 × 3 × 3.
> b. False, because the two products are equal. 9 × 3 is the same as 3 × 3 × 3. You just decomposed the 9 into 3 × 3 before multiplying by the other 3.
> c. True, because when you multiply two factors together, you will get a smaller product than when you multiply three factors together.
> d. True, because the product of 9 × 3 is less than the product of 3 × 3 × 3.
>
> Now, you will try it yourself. Determine if the equation below is true or false. If it is true, solve the problem and explain how you know it is correct. If it is false, explain why it is wrong, solve it correctly, and explain how you know it is now correct.
>
> $$2 \times 2 \times 3 < 4 \times 3$$

Upper Elementary

In the science classroom, you can ask students to design a bridge and justify its quality.

> Build a bridge. Based on what we have been learning in class, build the strongest bridge possible using items you can find in our classroom. When you present your bridge, prove to the rest of your classmates why it is strong.

Here's an upper elementary social studies example, in which students must take their learning to a new level in a dinner party. It is particularly elevated by relating inventions to our current society.

> Imagine a dinner party with esteemed guests such as Benjamin Franklin, Thomas Edison, Marie Curie, George Washington Carver, the Wright brothers, and Alexander Graham Bell. Using our texts and lessons on inventors, write a script in which these historical figures would discuss their inventions. Choose a character and role-play this scenario, thinking about what your inventor would say about the other inventions and about how his invention impacted society.

A terrific productive struggle activity involves making arguments, then justifying the argument with real-life examples.

> Ask students to write a persuasive letter to the principal, asking him or her to change a school rule they want to change. In addition to stating their position, they should provide specific reasons for the change as well as real-life examples for each reason.

Grade Four

Now, let's look at a reading and writing example that requires students to evaluate conflict, both in the story and in real life, write how they would handle the story, compare that to the character's probably actions, and justify who would handle it better.

> Think about the main character. How did the main character handle conflict in the book? Explain how you could have handled the same conflict differently and how the story would change based on that. Think of another conflict you have experienced. How did you handle it? Based on what happened in the story, how would the main character handle it? Justify whether you or the character handled it better.

Look at this science example, in which students write an argument and propose a solution.

> Research your chosen region in your state. Think of a realistic change that might happen to affect the plants and animals in your environment. Write an argument with evidence discussing what would happen to the other populations of animals. You must also propose how these cited problems could be fixed.

Grade Five

An excellent science activity for fifth graders involves water filters. Notice that students are designing filters, and then justifying whether or not it is effective.

> Students are provided a limited set of materials and are asked to design an effective water filter. In order to ensure the task is at an appropriate level, do not include some common filters, such as a mesh screen. This will push students beyond a basic water filter. Finally, students should write a short essay justifying why their water filer is effective.

In a reading activity, students read an article about the Lusitania in 1915.

> Discuss the roles of the British and the Germans in the Lusitania disaster. Were the British, Germans, both, or neither in the wrong? Provide a detailed explanation with evidence to support your answer.

Now we'll look at three additional subjects, art, technology, and physical education. Notice in the first art example, students must analyze both their own art and a piece by Jackson Pollock to reflect on the similarities and differences.

Art (Grades 3 and Up)

Create your own Jackson Pollack piece of art (https://jacksonpollock.org). Then, write a reflection explaining why your art is like Jackson Pollack's.

Upper Elementary Art

Next, notice the critical role of evaluation in this art activity, which is appropriate for grades 4 and up. Students are also required to move beyond opinions to support of their opinions.

> Students move through an art gallery of work created by their classmates. Each student chooses one piece of art and writes a short critique. The critique must include the student's opinion of the artwork, support of the opinion based on the lesson taught by the teacher and the student's own experiences, and recommendations for improvement.

Technology (All Grades)

After our class online visit to the zoo, design a t-shirt about your trip. You'll need to use some of the following skills: save pictures you find online, cut and paste, image editing, inserting text, and image design. When you present your t-shirt to the class, justify your choices for the shirt based on your learning and your own experiences.

Physical Education (All Grades)

Finally, here's a physical education activity that is appropriate for all grades. Rather than simply demonstrating a skill, students are identifying whether or not the skill is correct, and justifying their choice.

> For a specific physical education concept, such as throwing a ball, ask students to do the following:
>
> Demonstrate the skill twice for your partner (or the class). Ask your partner to identify whether you did the skill correctly or incorrectly. If correct, ask your partner to explain why it is correct. If incorrect, ask him or her to explain why it is not correct and then explain how to correct it.

Each of these examples provides a picture of productive struggle.

What Is the Difference Between an Explanation and a Justification?

A key difference in work that requires productive struggle is explanation vs. justification. Too often, we ask students to explain a statement or explain why they think something is true. When you explain something, you are simply giving your opinion, although you may give an example. It's perfectly appropriate, but usually does not require productive struggle to produce it. On the other hand, when you justify something, you state an argument and base your thoughts or analysis on specific evidence from the text or lesson. You link that evidence to your comment or analysis. The next natural step is to go beyond the text into other learning or real-life. Let's look at some samples that show the difference.

Explanation vs. Justification	
Explanation	*Justification*
Why is X the main character?	Justify your choice of main character using specific actions he or she takes and how those actions reflect a main character rather than a supporting character.
Which story do you like better and why?	Explain your choice using specific examples from the text and why it links to your life (be specific).
How did you solve the problem?	Justify your answer using what you have learned in class and using math words.
Solve the problem. Explain your answer.	Samir and Angel lost 13 teeth total. How do you know this is correct? Use math words to answer.
Why is a roller coaster fun?	What makes a roller coaster fun? Justify how specific elements of the roller coaster add to the enjoyment of the ride.
How did you find your answer?	Justify each step that you used to solve the problem, using what you know about math.
Why did your experiment work?	Explain why your experiment did or did not work. Your explanation should be based on facts you learned in our class and from additional research and should specifically be linked to aspects of your experiment.
Why?	Explain to me why you think that based on the book we read.

Notice that the word itself (explain or justify) is not as important as what the students are asked to do. In the justification column, students are moving beyond their opinion by providing specific information for their thoughts. You can use a simple question such as why, but you want to push students to move beyond the answer to a higher level.

A Final Note

Providing tasks and assignments that are at an appropriate level is a critical part of the productive struggle process. Theories such as Vygotsky's Zone of Proximal Development and Flow from Mihaly Csikszentmihalyi are helpful, as is choosing a suitable level of text. The characteristics of the task matter, as does requiring students to justify responses rather than simply explaining an answer.

Points to Ponder

1. How will you use the concepts of flow or the zone of proximal development?
2. How does the information related to levelled text impact your classroom?
3. What specific task characteristics are most applicable to your instruction?
4. How can you reword one of your questions to include justification?

Continue the Learning

Use the QR Code to access videos for your own use or for group professional development.

5

Scaffolding for Productive Struggle

General Scaffolding for Productive Struggle

Scaffolding is an integral part of productive struggle. There is a balance—supporting students without solving problems for them. This chapter has two main parts. First, we'll look at some general scaffolding strategies that are useful during productive struggle. Some may be used prior to the task; others may be used as needed during the task. You'll be the best person to determine that. Also, some scaffolding may be needed for certain students, rather than everyone. The goal is to scaffold when needed, but not if it takes away the productive part of the struggle. In the first part of the chapter, we'll discuss six general strategies.

> How to Scaffold the "Learning Together" Process
> Discourse During Productive Struggle
> Teaching Students to Activate Prior Knowledge
> Modeling Processes for Productive Struggle
> Supportive Questioning During Productive Struggle
> Providing Resources for Students

Then, in the second part, we'll revisit each of the productive struggle tasks from Chapter 4, this time with descriptions and examples of appropriate scaffolding.

How to Scaffold the "Learning Together" Process

Group work is one of the most effective ways to help students learn, especially in a productive learning setting. It can increase student motivation and is an important life skill. When I was teaching, some of my students didn't like to work in groups. They complained every day until I brought in a newspaper article that said the number one reason people were fired from their jobs was that they couldn't get along with their coworkers. That was an eye-opener for my students.

If you are going to ask students to work together in productive struggle, one of the ways to scaffold their success is to teach them how to work together. Let's consider five areas related to group work.

Areas Related to Group Work

Structures During Productive Struggle

Roles for Group Members

Rules for Working Together

Discourse During Productive Struggle

Questions to Prompt Discourse

Structures During Productive Struggle

First, determine how you want to organize your groups. Do you want students to work in pairs, groups of four, or some other organization? Will your students stay in the same group for a long period of time? I find that balance is important, and the task for productive struggle will often dictate what you should decide. For example, sometimes the task is most appropriate for partners, other times a larger group of four or five is effective.

I also think students should learn to work with the same people over time as well as learning to work with a variety of people, and they should not be limited to working with the same students all the time. In my classroom, I used groups of four for some activities and pairs for other activities. I switched my students around often enough that they rarely complained about other group members. They knew that I expected them to learn to work with everyone and that they would be grouped with someone else later.

Roles for Group Members

A critical step is structuring your group activity. Create an activity that requires each student to contribute to the task. It's important to assign roles for your students, although you may want students within a group to choose their roles. The roles may change depending on your assignment. For example, if students are working on a science experiment, you will need a safety monitor and a materials manager. However, if your project is developing visual model, you might prefer an artist.

Sample Roles and Responsibilities

Facilitator—Leader of the group; facilitates action
Recorder—Records comments and/or work
Reporter—Reports work to the entire group
Materials Manager—Collects and distributes materials
Timekeeper—Keeps the group working within time limits
Technology Manager—Coordinates technology use
Encourager—Encourages others
Summarizer—Summarizes work and may report to the class
Fact checker—Checks work from group; researches facts
Reflector—Reflects on comments from group, asks probing questions
Designer—Designs the project
Creator—Creates or builds the design

I encourage you to rotate the roles within the team for different assignments so that one or two students do not dominate the group activities. You should also take time to teach students about their roles and responsibilities. This will ensure that the group process doesn't interfere with their productive struggle.

Rules for Working Together

In addition to your standard classroom rules, you may need a couple of simple rules that are specific to productive struggle group activities. I found that I needed to discuss my expectations for the noise level of the classroom. For example, I wanted my students to talk to each other. But they needed to talk to their group members, not the entire class. You might come up with a catchy way to describe an appropriate noise level, such as "Bees Buzz." Bees buzz when they are being productive (making honey), but they don't shout. I was in another classroom in which the teacher talked about using your "12-inch voice." Her students knew that meant that people within a foot (within the group) should be able hear you, but not those outside the group (more than a foot away).

I also used a rule called "ask three before me." This one works when your students are in groups of four. It simply means that a student should ask his or her group members for help before asking the teacher. This encourages students to look to each other for support instead of always looking to the teacher first. It's up to you to decide what rules you need in your classroom. Be sure that your students understand your expectations, and monitor the groups continuously to ensure that all students have an opportunity to participate. Here are sample rules I used.

Sample Group Rules

Respect Each Other

Listen Carefully

Help Each Other

Bees Buzz

Take Turns

Ask Three Before Me

Finally, you may want to use talking chips, a strategy in which you give each student three chips or tokens. Each time a student speaks, he or she must turn in his or her chip (in a bag in the center of the group). When each student is out of chips, they are not allowed to talk until all other students have turned in their chips. This ensures participation from all students.

Discourse During Productive Struggle

Elements of Successful Discourse

Successful discourse is critical to productive struggle. Too often, we accept what is simply noise—students talking, perhaps off-topic, often over each other. That's not discourse. Discourse is "classroom talk." It is on-topic, it uses academic vocabulary, and students listen just as much as they talk. Let's look at the 9 characteristics of effective discourse.

> Disagreements are handled respectfully
> Indicators of success are well defined
> Students participate equally and equitably
> Clear directions are given
> Open-ended opportunities are provided
> Use of wait time and scaffolding is appropriate
> Raise the level of talk with academic vocabulary
> Students ask questions in addition to answering them
> Everyone is successful

In the following table, you can find a simple self-assessment for students to use regarding discourse.

Lower Grades Academic Conversations Expectations			
	Beginning	*Moving Forward*	*Expert*
Remarks	I shared my thoughts	I shared my thoughts with examples and reasoning	I shared my thoughts with reasoning and asked my classmates for their feedback
Responses	I listened to others' ideas	I listened to others' ideas and responded with my thoughts	I listened to others' ideas, clarified what I heard, and connected by responding with my thoughts
Reflection	I thought about what I heard my classmates say	I considered what my classmates had to say and looked for connections to my ideas	With an open mind, I internalized what my classmates were saying and used it to grow my understanding

Questions to Prompt Discourse During Productive Struggle

It's helpful to provide starter questions to help students discuss their productive struggle tasks.

Starter Questions
To Prompt More Thinking:
♦ You are on the right track. Tell us more.
♦ You are onto something. Keep going.
♦ The teacher said there is no right answer, so what would be your best answer?
To Fortify or Justify a Response
♦ What is your opinion about . . . ?
♦ Why is what you said important?
♦ Why do you think that?
♦ Explain how you got that answer.
To See Others' Points of View
♦ How is what you are thinking different from me?
♦ Do you see another way to do this?
To Consider Consequences
♦ How can we apply this to real life?

Starter Questions
♦ What did you learn in another lesson that we can connect this too?
♦ How else can we use this?

Source: adapted from http://ptgmedia.pearsoncmg.com/images/9780205627585/downloads/ Echevarria_math_Ch1_TheAcademicLanguageofMathematics.pdf

Here's another set for specific subject areas.

Sample Question Starters			
Language Arts	*Math*	*Science*	*Social Studies*
Which character . . . ?	When I compare . . . ?	Which reaction . . . ?	What led to . . . ?
Why did . . . ?	When I order . . . ?	If I did this again would . . . ?	Which events were . . . ?
If . . . ?	What information . . . ?	Why did this . . . ?	How did they . . . ?
Which clues . . . ?	Which phrases . . . ?	How did this . . . ?	Why did they . . . ?
Where did . . . ?	How do I . . . ?	How might the results change if . . . ?	How might things have been different if . . . ?
Which word or phrase . . . ?	I wonder if another solution . . . ?		
What event . . . ?			

Teaching Students to Activate Prior Knowledge

Helping students activate their prior knowledge can help them be more successful during productive struggle. You can use an anticipation guide, drawing guide, or K-W-L.

Mathematics Example		
Agree/Disagree Before the Activity	*Content*	*Agree/Disagree After the Activity*
	A square has four sides.	
	A triangle has two sides.	
	A rectangle has four sides.	

In this sample, younger students draw what they know, then revise their drawings after the lesson.

Knowledge Drawings	
Draw What I Think I Know About the Topic	*Revise Your Drawing After the Lesson*

K-W-L Charts

Probably the most common method of activating students' prior knowledge that I see in classrooms today is a K-W-L chart. During a K-W-L activity, you ask the students what they already know about a topic (K) or what they think they know about it. Next, you ask what they want to know (W). Then, you teach the lesson and ask them what they learned (L). You can also add an H—"How Can We Learn This" to create a K-W-H-L organizer.

K-W-H-L Chart			
K (what I know or think I know)	W (what I want to learn)	H (how I can learn this)	L (what I learned)

I particularly like the KWHL for productive struggle. Students can use the graphic to reflect on their knowledge and also plan a strategy for learning.

Modeling Processes for Productive Struggle

How often are your students confused? Mine were confused more often that I'd like to remember. Some of your students, particularly your struggling learners, need to understand what is happening in your head. They need you to show them what you think and how you think. Although important throughout your instruction, it's particularly important with productive struggle.

Modeling Thinking

If your students are working with online resources, we may need to model how to effectively "read" a website.

> When I look up information on the internet, I make sure I pay attention to the right material. I look for the headline, which is usually bigger or in a darker text. Then I look for the reading below the headline. That is the main focus of my reading. If there are pictures or videos, I ignore them unless I can see they specifically help me with the reading. I also ignore all the ads.

You can follow the same process with any instruction.

1st Grade Problem Think Aloud

(Note: Teacher should also write and draw this out for students)

Okay, I see the problem says *13 minus 8*. That means I am starting with **13**, and I need to take **8** away.

Let me think . . . I know 13 is a **teen number**, so that's **10 and 3 more**.

If I take away 8, that's almost like taking away **10**, but 8 is a little less than 10. Hmm . . . maybe I can break it apart to make it easier.

I know **13 − 3 = 10**, but I'm supposed to take away 8. I've only taken away 3 so far, so I still need to take away **5 more** (because 8 is 3 + 5).

So now I have **10 − 5 = 5**.

Let me check: I started with 13. I took away 3—that got me to 10. Then I took away 5 more—that got me to 5.

So **13 minus 8 equals 5**.

I'll double-check with counting backwards to make sure I'm right. Starting at 13. . .12, 11, 10, 9, 8, 7, 6, 5—that was 8 hops backwards, and I landed on **5** again!

Yes—the answer is **5**.

Adapted From ChatGPT Example

See how simple it is? In fact, it's so automatic for us, we assume everyone else would know how to think through that process. Your strong students will be able to do that in their heads, but your struggling students will not understand. That's why it's important to model your thinking as needed during the productive struggle process.

Modeling With Video

Jessica Neuberger uses modeling to prepare students for their first student-led portfolio assessment conferences. As she explains:

> I recorded a sample interview to give the students a good idea of what to expect. When the class viewed the sample interview, I would stop the video after each question, have the students repeat each question to me and then they would write it down. The second time through, we watched the whole interview with no interruptions. Then we discussed it. When I interviewed the students throughout the next week, they were prepared to share their work with me, offer me their opinions of their strengths and weaknesses, and we were able to set a goal for the next part of the year.

Because she knew this would be challenging for her students, she modeled the entire process for them and then provided scaffolded instruction to ensure their success. What I like about this is that the video could be available as students need it during the productive struggle process.

Supportive Questioning During Productive Struggle

One way to scaffold questions is by using other questions that lead to the answer. For example, simply asking "Where will a seed grow best?" can be supported with questions such as: "What do plants need to grow?" "Does light matter?" "How can you find out?"

The following is an example of how supporting questions can be used to guide students in determining an overall theme in *The Girl Who Never Makes Mistakes* by Mark Pett.

Essential Question: How Do People Show Courage When They Face Challenges?

Scaffolding questions:
1. What challenge does Beatrice face at the beginning of the story?
2. How does Beatrice *feel* about the possibility of making a mistake?
3. What kinds of things does she *do* so she won't make mistakes? What does that tell us about her?

4. When Beatrice finally makes a mistake on stage, how does she react at first?
5. What choice does Beatrice make after her mistake—and why does that take courage?
6. How are her feelings different *before* and *after* she makes a mistake?
7. What lesson is Beatrice starting to learn about being brave when challenges happen?

It's important to note that these questions don't provide the answer; they ask students to look for more narrow information that leads to the broader question. That's critical during productive struggle—you want to provide support without providing the answer to your students.

Providing Resources for Students

Providing ready-to-use resources is also important. Consider what students might need during the productive struggle process. Let's look at five types of resources.

> Friendly Dictionaries
> Word Walls
> Guide-o-Ramas
> Leveled Texts
> Graphic Organizers

First, I particularly like having friendly dictionaries available for students. When I was teaching young students, having a primary dictionary was critical. The one we used was organized by themes, such as farm or ocean, and the words and pictures all related to the theme. There are a wide range available now, both in print and online, such as the Oxford Children's Dictionary or the WILD dictionary for K–2 by Wordsmyth. I also like the Collins COBUILD Dictionary, which uses more student-friendly definitions.

If you teach something other than reading/language arts/English, much of your vocabulary is specialized, which likely has a unique meaning. Therefore, you need something different.

Math	Science
Amathsdictionaryforkids.com Mathisfun.com (K–12) Mathwords.com Wolfram Math World	World of Science Enchanted Learning (includes specialized dictionaries such as astronomy and botany) Visionlearning Glossary
Social Studies	Others
Ancient History Encyclopedia Online Dictionary of the Social Sciences Geography Dictionary and Glossary (ISTE)	Netlingo (technology definitions) Sportsdefinitions.com Museum of Modern Art dictionary Naxos.com (music) Inc. Com Encyclopedia (business)

Word Walls

Another resource is word walls, which have been in favor for years. For example, when I was teaching I posted new spelling words on the ceiling. Finally, a student noticed, and they were intrigued that I not only posted the words, but left them up in case they needed help. My purpose, in part, was to teach them to find information when they needed it instead of just memorizing words. Ironically, they studied harder knowing they had extra assistance available.

I recommend having a specific word wall for your current instruction, including the task for productive struggle. Whether you are teaching vowel sounds, fractions, particles, types of government, or elements of art, there are key words and concepts your students need to know. You can post all the words in advance and refer to them throughout your lessons or post them as you teach. Be sure to place your words in a prominent place in your classroom.

Other Tips for Word Walls

Be sure your lettering is large enough to be seen throughout the room. Be careful with colors—yellow looks bright, but it doesn't work well for the words themselves.

Put your word wall where students can see it clearly—that may be lower for younger students, higher for older students.
Add pictures for English learners.
Remove words once they are generally understood. Make room for new words.

You can also use personal word walls for students or groups. Using file folders, notebooks, or shared documents, students develop their own word walls based on the task, your instruction and guidance. I like using post-it notes for the words so students can rearrange them and remove words as needed.

Sample Personal or Group Word Wall	
General Words for the Topic	*Words for this Task*
Words I'm Working On	*Other Words*

Guide-o-Rama

Whether you are asking students to read a portion of text, you will also want to model your thinking. It's important to provide a guide. Otherwise, students won't know what to look for. These can be detailed, or more general. If you blend a think-aloud with study guide notes, it is very effective for students to use in group, partner, or individual work. Guide-o-Ramas combine a study guide with a think-aloud.

\	*Science Guide-O-Rama Air Pollution*	
Section	*Tip*	*Student Comment*
Picture at the top of the page and "What Is Air Pollution?" section	This section is important. I should read the title and first section to see if the article will help me learn about air pollution: What can I assume from the title? Do I understand the definition?	
Natural Causes of Air Pollution and Human Causes of Air Pollution	In these two sections of the article, causes of air pollution are listed. Did I already know all of these causes? Are there causes that are new to me? In a section about natural causes; forest fires are highlighted in blue; this means I should explore this link. It might provide more information about natural causes of air pollution.	
Effects on the Environment	In this section, there is a bulleted list, and after each bullet, an effect is listed. I should read these sections carefully and write a summary of each one. There are also more words and phrases in blue highlight. I should explore carbon, carbon cycle, and ozone because we talked about these in class. Add these words to my notebook.	

Science Guide-O-Rama Air Pollution		
Section	*Tip*	*Student Comment*
Picture with Caption: Smog in the city makes it hard to breathe and see	After seeing the picture in the last section, I realized: I need to read a little more because this sounds like another effect on the environment. Write about two ways air pollution affects the environment in my own words.	

Source: adapted from www.ducksters.com/scienceenvironment/air_pollution.php

Below, you'll find tips for building a guide-o-rama, which should only be used when students have moved beyond productive struggle to frustration. Use them judiciously. Also, for young students, I've found it more effective to give them the steps one at a time, rather than all at once.

How to Build a Guide-O-Rama

1. Identify a chunk of content you need students to read. Guide-o-ramas should be used with challenging texts that you anticipate students will struggle with.

2. Determine guiding questions that will help them process key portions of the text, similar to what you would use in a traditional study guide.

3. Add think-aloud comments, such as "Notice that on page 56, there is a box of math or science symbols. When I see a box of text in the margin, I pay special attention since it usually contains important information." These are typically questions and/or statements that you would verbally use to model your thinking for students.

4. Use visuals that will help students remember the content. For example, if students are reading about the Pythagorean Theorem, you might put each question in a right triangle.

5. Keep in mind that your goal is twofold: help students process and understand the complex text and move toward independence in learning.

Providing Layered Text

A particular concern in the upper elementary classroom occurs when students cannot read grade-level text. Sometimes you must start with easier text in order to build to more complex text, which will deepen understanding. One strategy for supporting students during productive struggle who are not reading at grade level is "layering meaning." This strategy can be used for any student who cannot yet read the grade-level or assigned text material because it allows students to read another text on the same topic that is written at an easier level. Students read that selection first to build their own prior knowledge and vocabulary; then they can go back and read the more complex text with your support. It's an excellent strategy, one that encourages high levels of challenge because students move beyond the easier text, but one that requires texts at differing levels. A variety of websites provide leveled texts for your use.

Sources for Leveled Text

**Right now, unless noted, these are free, but they may add premium items or add a fee at a later time.

Reading A to Z (https://www.readinga-z.com/books/leveled-books/) provides a variety of books and passages. KidsNews (https://www.kidsnews.com.au) is a terrific site in Australia that is designed for kids and their parents.

CommonLit (www.commonlit.org), News in Levels (http://www.newsinlevels.com), and FortheTeachers (http://www.fortheteachers.org/reading_skills/) also provide varying levels of an article or text. For the teachers has science, health, and other topics, but information is language arts oriented.

Reading Vine (https://www.readingvine.com/passages/skill/) provides text by levels.

Reading is Fundamental (https://www.rif.org/literacy-central/collections/leveled-reading-passages) provides leveled reading passages.

TweenTribune (http://tweentribune.com) is produced by the Smithsonian. It is now archived, but may be helpful

Readworks (http://www.readworks.org) is a little different—they do texts, including paired texts, but they do **not** provide differing levels of the same text.

- Text Compactor (http://www.textcompactor.com) lets you paste text into it and then automatically summarizes it (with a customized setting you control).
- Rewordify (http://rewordify.com) allows a teacher or student to paste text into the screen, and it will identify challenging words and replace them with explanations.
- Diffit is an AI tool (free for most features; premium available) which allows you to enter text and ask for differing levels.
- Paraphrase (https://paraphrasetool.com/modes/shorten-paraphrasing-tool?gclid=CjwKCAiA04arBhAkEi-wAuNOsIsINpv_vaLwLiaY3beAl06Qji80Eyt8NrvaQmUeb4cg-1C2iZAy5CZBoC2s4QAvD_BwE) does exactly that—generally shortening the text.

Graphic Organizers

Graphic organizers are an excellent resource for students. They help students organize their information visually and chunk information that might be overwhelming. Having graphic organizers available tied to the productive struggle task is an excellent resource. Later in the chapter, you'll see specific examples tied to the tasks from Chapter 4. Let's look at several general samples.

This sample allows students to build connections to their learning.

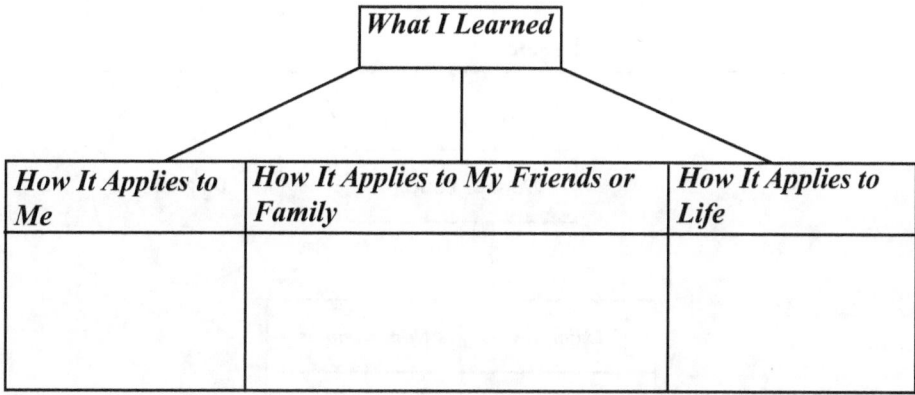

If you are showing a video, having a viewing guide is helpful. The guide is simple, but keep in mind it is building to a complex task and is only providing support.

Broader Viewing Guide

Viewing Guide for _____	
What are the key points in the video?	
What examples are given for each of the main points?	
What questions do you have?	
What is the most important thing you learned from the video?	

I particularly like a graphic organizer to understand vocabulary.

Vocabulary Graphic Organizer

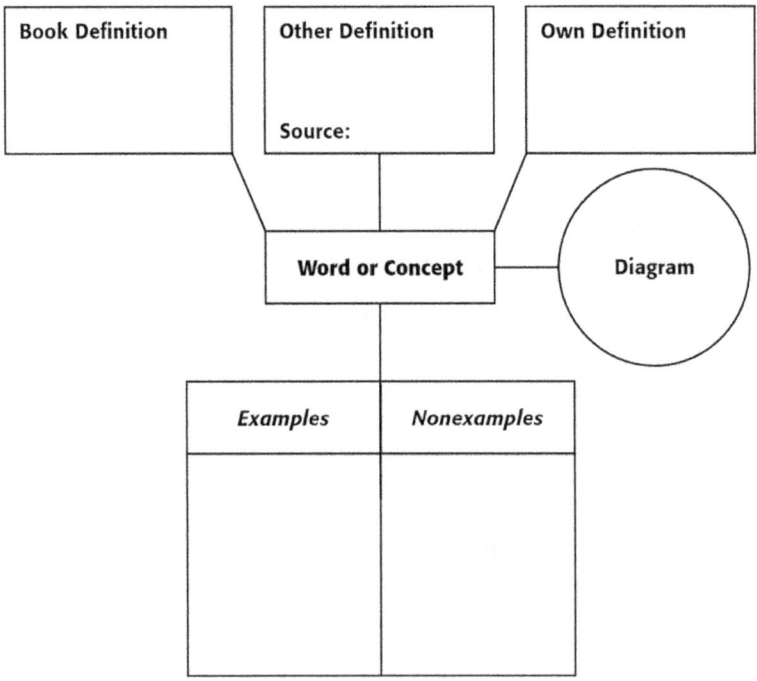

The next sample asks students to apply information from a non-fiction book about bees to the book *The Queen Ants Birthday*.

Worker Bees	Guard Bees

↓ ↓

What They Do For Queen Bee	What They Do For Queen Bee

Finally, a simple organizer helps student determine why math problems do or do not make sense.

Does or Does Not Make Sense			
	Problem	This Makes Sense Because . . .	This Doesn't Make Sense Because . . .
1.			
2.			
3.			

Teaching Students to Self-Scaffold

One of the best ways to scaffold learning through productive struggle is to teach students to self-scaffold. Ideally, anytime you use a scaffolding strategy you use it in a way that teaches students how to independently use it. However, there are three specific ways to teach students to self-scaffold.

Question Starters

First, keep a bank of question starters in a readily available place for students. Earlier in the chapter I provided samples you can use. For younger students, you may want to use simple, one-word questions.

One Word Questions		
Who?	What?	When?
Where?	Why?	How?

Graphic Organizers

Next, graphic organizers are a key resource for students. Although there are times you will want to provide an organizer designed for the specific task, there are also general organizers you may keep available for students at all times. Giving them tips for choosing a graphic organizer is helpful.

Choosing a Graphic Organizer	
Question	*Type of Graphic Organizer*
Do you need to summarize 2 topics?	T-Chart
Do you need to compare and contrast?	Venn Diagram
Do you need to summarize information for different topics?	Semantic Feature Analysis
Do you want to describe a sequence?	Sequence Chart

Determining When I Need Help

Finally, you want to teach students to scaffold for themselves before asking you for help. I used the following reminders to help them make that decision.

	How to Get Help
Try It On Your Own	What exactly do I need help with? Have I learned something similar before? What have I learned that will help me? Is there anything on our walls that will help? Is there anything in our classroom resource kit that can help?
Work with Others	Can anyone in my group help me? Can we work together to solve the problem? Do we need to ask someone not in our group? Who might know the answer?
Ask the Teacher	I've tried on my own, and I've asked other people. Can you help me now?

Applying Scaffolding to Productive Struggle Activities

Now, let's look at how scaffolding applies to particular productive struggle activities. We're going to return to each of the tasks from Chapter 4, adding specific scaffolding strategies. At times, I'll simply note a strategy, such as modeling. Other times, such as using graphic organizers, I'll provide a sample for your use.

Kindergarten

> Students take turns playing the Red Herring Game. Each group stands up, states a letter (A–Z) then shares three words. Other students identify the word that does not start with the stated letter.

Ideally, you would model this activity prior to student work. This allows students to see your expectation. Also, you might provide an alphabet chart students could use to organize their words.

Alphabet Chart					
A	B	C	D	E	F
G	H	I	J	K	L
M	N	O	P	Q	R
S	T	U	V	W	X
Y	Z				

Here is another example.

Students design a rule to solve a classroom problem.

With this task, a graphic organizer is helpful. They can write or draw their responses.

Solving a Classroom Problem		
Problem	Why?	How to Solve

Grade One

James and Marissa both solved the problem below.
They got two different answers. Who is correct?
Justify your answer.

For this math problem, modeling all or part of the process is helpful. Additionally, using guided questions with students may help them work through their struggles.

Scaffolding for Productive Struggle ◆ 115

> **Guided Questions**
>
> Would it help to use blocks to do the math?
>
> How do the pictures help you solve the math?

Now, let's look at another example.

> The teacher provides pictures from a story. After sequencing the pictures, students explain how the scene changed over time. They also elaborate on their explanation by justifying the changes with specific examples from the story.

For this sequence activity, you might use question prompts or provide a T-chart for students.

> **Question Prompts**
>
> What does each picture show?
>
> Does it help to think about the change for each picture?
>
> How exactly does the picture show the change(s)?

T-Chart to Justify Changes	
Change	*Example*

Primary Grades

After the class reads *The Frog Book* and *The Frog Who Lost His Croak*.

How was the frog like the frogs in the first book? Was he like a real frog, or was he made-up?

Why do you think that?

If the frog who lost his croak met the frogs in *The Frog Book*, what would he ask them? Why?

What would the frogs in both books tell a baby frog are the most important things he or she should know in life?

There are three possible scaffolding activities in this frog activity. First, you may want to chunk the questions, allowing students to focus on one at a time. Next, it is helpful to model how to answer a "why" question. Finally, a semantic feature analysis can help students organize their information.

Semantic Feature Analysis			
	Basic Facts About Frogs	*Where Frogs Live*	*What Frogs Eat*
The Frog Book			
The Frog Who Lost His Croak			

Here is another example.

> We have been reading and talking about the adventures of Tum Tum and Nutmeg. Living in a world where everything is considerably larger than them, we see their unique perspective on places and events that are ordinary to us. Being "small" in your own world, how can you connect with these mice? Are there times when you wish you were bigger or older or that your voice was heard more clearly? Are there times when you "see" things differently than the adults around you? What would you say to the adults in your life about the way you see things?
>
> Now let's read *Clifford, the Big Red Dog*. How is Clifford's view of the world very different than Emily Elizabeth's? What's different about seeing things from a much larger point of view? Imagine that you have been sent to a deserted island where everything is very, very small. Your view of the world would be quite different than the little people that live there. Using pictures and or/words, describe how you might see things from a different perspective. Create a video introducing yourself to the people who live there, explaining how you see things differently.

This activity is another one in which it is helpful to chunk the questions. Sometimes students can become overwhelmed with the amount of questioning in this task. Next, graphic organizers for each book continue to help students chunk information.

Tum Tum and Nutmeg	
Tum Tum and Nutmeg: Adventures Beyond Nutmouse Hall	
Are Tum Tum and Nutmeg big or small?	How does being big or small make a difference to them? Give examples.

Clifford the Big Red Dog	
Is Clifford big or small?	How does his size make Clifford's life different? Give examples.
Is Elizabeth big or small?	How does her size make her life different from Clifford's? Give examples.

Grade Two

Students study community workers such as a police officer, firefighter, librarian, nurse, teacher, plumber, bus driver, or mayor. At the end of the unit, each student identifies a worker's job they would like, and they complete a job application.

Name_____Date of Application _____

Which of the classroom jobs are you applying for? Write the job title on the line below.
_____

Why are you interested in this job?
_____

Analyze and describe how you are qualified for the job. You must include specific experiences you have had to prepare you and specific traits you have that qualify you. All examples must include why each prepares you for the job, linking to what you have learned about the job.
_____
_____
_____

First, this is another instance in which you may want to chunk the questions, allowing students to focus on one at a time. Next, a graphic organizer will help students structure their information.

Jobs Graphic Organizer	
Job you want to apply for	
Traits needed in the job	How I have the traits
Things I have done that will help me in this job	How each will help me in this job

---

Name: _____   Date: _____

Force and Motion

Obtain, evaluate, and communicate information to explain the effect of a force (a push or a pull) in the movement of an object (changes in speed or direction).

a. Plan and carry out an investigation to demonstrate how pushing and pulling on an object affects the motion of the object.

b. Design a device to change the speed or direction of an object.

c. Record and analyze data to decide if a design solution works as intended to change the speed or direction of an object with a force (a push or pull). Based on what you have learned in class, your data, and your life, why does your device do what I asked you to do?

In this investigation, there are two graphic organizers that are helpful. First is a visual to help students with the overall design. Next is a data collection chart.

Graphic Organizer for Design	
What is your object?	
What device will you use to change the speed or direction of the object?	
How do you think the device will change the speed of the object?	How do you think the device will change the direction of the object?

Data Record Sheet		
Attempt	*Did you push or pull?*	*What changed?*

Grade Three

> As the culmination of a ten-day unit, students create a school on Mars to support the colonists' lives there. Students must figure out what the curriculum should be, the physical design of the school, and the design of the outside garden. It's important to note the curriculum needs to prepare students for jobs and real life on Mars. Specific reasons for each choice should be explained.

This task lends itself nicely to using graphic organizers to compile information. Again, they helps students chunk the material to be used.

Life on Mars		
Describe what you know about life on Mars		
School Curriculum	School Design	Garden Design
How does your school prepare students for jobs and life on Mars?		

Life on Mars	
Life on Mars	What to Teach in School
Life on Mars	How to Build the School
Life on Mars	How to Design Garden

Here is another example.

Third Grade Mathematics Unit 3

Name:
Date:

Directions: Read each question two times. Please CIRCLE the correct answer for each question. Show your math thinking for each problem. It's okay to write on this test!

1. Jermaine was asked to determine if the equation below was true or false, and then he had to explain why. Which answer choice was his explanation?

    $$3 \times 3 \times 3 > 9 \times 3$$

    A. False, because the product of 9×3 is greater than the product of $3 \times 3 \times 3$.
    B. False, because the two products are equal. 9×3 is the same as $3 \times 3 \times 3$. You just decomposed the 9 into 3×3 before multiplying by the other 3.
    C. True, because when you multiply two factors together, you will get a smaller product than when you multiply three factors together.
    D. True, because the product of 9×3 is less than the product of $3 \times 3 \times 3$.

2. Now, you will try it yourself. Determine if the equation below is true or false. If it is true, solve the problem and explain how you know it is correct. If it's false, explain why it is wrong, solve it correctly, and explain how you know it is now correct.

    $$2 \times 2 \times 3 < 4 \times 3$$

Although this math problem looks simple, the task is actually complex. For questions one and two, it's helpful to break down the steps to assist in solving the problem. This leads to a second option, which is modeling how to analyze the answers. You may also offer students highlighters to use to color code the specific math in the answers.

Upper Elementary

Build a bridge. Based on what we have been learning in class, build the strongest bridge possible using items you can find in our classroom. When you present your bridge, prove to the rest of your classmates why it is strong.

The heart of this task is choosing the strongest items to build the bridge. Students may find a graphic organizer to brainstorm items to use helpful.

Choosing Items for a Strong Bridge		
Item	*Strong or Weak*	*Rank Your Choices*

Final Items to Use:

Why I Built a Strong Bridge:

This example helps students use a semantic feature analysis.

> Imagine a dinner party with esteemed guests such as Benjamin Franklin, Thomas Edison, Marie Curie, George Washington Carver, the Wright brothers, and Alexander Graham Bell. Using our texts and lessons on inventors, write a script in which these historical figures would discuss their inventions. Choose a character and role-play this scenario, thinking about what your inventor would say about the other inventions and about how his invention impacted society.

The dinner party activity encompasses a large amount of information. If students are overwhelmed, a semantic feature analysis can help them synthesize their learning.

Semantic Feature Analysis About Inventors				
	Invention(s)	*Purpose of Invention*	*Impact of Invention*	*A Quote from the Inventor(s)*
Benjamin Franklin				
Thomas Edison				
Marie Curie				
George Washington Carver				
The Wright Brothers				
Alexander Graham Bell				

You might also model how to write a script, as well as using a checklist for a role-play scenario.

Be Sure to Include in Your Script

- My invention and its purpose
- Why I developed it
- My opinion of others' inventions
- How my invention impacted history
- How my invention is impacting life today

Ask students to write a persuasive letter to the principal, asking him or her to change a school rule they want to change. In addition to stating their position, they should provide specific reasons for the change as well as real-life examples for each reason.

There are two key scaffolds that are helpful in persuasive letters. First, you might use a checklist for persuasive letters. Then, a T-Chart of reasons and examples assists students in organizing their thoughts.

Be Sure to Include in Your Persuasive Letter

- State your position and the change you want
- Give reasons for the change
- Give a minimum of one example for each reason
- End with a strong conclusion

T-Chart of Reasons and Examples

Reason to Change Rule	Examples Why

Grades Four

> Think about the main character. How did the main character handle conflict in the book? Explain how you could have handled the same conflict differently and how the story would change based on that. Think of another conflict you have experienced. How did you handle it? Based on what happened in the story, how would the main character handle it? Justify whether you or the character handled it better.

While helping students analyze conflict, you may want to provide supportive questioning. Additionally, a graphic organizer for the questions and a T-chart are helpful as students process the task.

Conflict Graphic Organizer	
Conflict from the book	
How the main character handled the conflict	How I would have handled it
How the story would change if I handled it	
Conflict from my life:	

Conflict Graphic Organizer

How I handled it	How the main character would have handled it

Who would have handled it better? Why?

Conflict T-Chart for Comparison

How Main Character Handled Conflict	How I Would Handle It
How I Handled Conflict	How the Main Character Would Handle It

An additional example:

> Research your chosen region in your state. Think of a realistic change that might happen to affect the plants and animals in your environment. Write an argument with evidence discussing what would happen to the other populations of animals. You must also propose how these cited problems could be fixed.

When students are asked to research a topic, they may become overwhelmed and unable to find sources. A key scaffolding strategy is to help them narrow their sources, whether by giving them a range of resources, providing specific sources, or asking questions to help them think about sources (such as, "Have you thought about a video?"). You may also want to provide a graphic organizer for an argumentative essay.

Graphic Organizer for Argumentative Essay

Change That Is Occurring:

What Might Happen to Other Animals	Evidence

How to Fix These Problems:

Grade Five

> Students are provided a limited set of materials and are asked to design an effective water filter. In order to ensure the task is at an appropriate level, do not include some common filters, such as a mesh screen. This will push students beyond a basic water filter. Finally, students should write a short essay justifying why their water filer is effective.

There are two scaffolding resources that are helpful with this activity. First, students may benefit from a graphic organizer to help with the design. Second, a checklist for writing an essay will provide guidance if needed on the final part of the task.

Graphic Organizer for Designing Filter	
What are the characteristics of a filter?	
Materials Available	Helpful or Not? Why or Why Not?
Notebook Paper	
Paper Towels	
Plastic Cup	
Chalk	
Beanbag	
Rocks	
Sponge Pieces	

Graphic Organizer for Designing Filter	
Cloth	
Crayons	
Book	
Glue	
Sand	
Cotton Balls	
What we used to make a filter:	
Why our filter works:	

Checklist for Essay

> Be Sure to Include in Your Essay
>
> ♦ State your position and the change you want.
> ♦ Include how you designed your filter.
> ♦ Describe reasons your filter is effective.
> ♦ Give at least one specific example for each reason you gave.
> ♦ Finish with a strong conclusion summarizing your filter's effectiveness.
>
> Discuss the roles of the British and the Germans in the Lusitania disaster. Were the British, Germans, both, or neither, in the wrong? Provide a detailed explanation with evidence to support your answer.

The first support tool for this activity is a Guide-o-Rama for students who need the extra help processing the text.

Guide-o-Rama for Article on the Lusitania

What was the unique cargo carried by the Lusitania? Because it is different, I'm going to think about why it might make a difference to the passengers.

How do you feel about the German officers planning to destroy any ships that might help their enemies? That would be a tough decision. How would you make the decision whether or not to destroy a ship? What would you think about?

Wow! A German U-boat did shoot the Lusitania! I wonder if they knew ammunition was on board? Why do you think they shot the boat?

A lot of people were killed, including Americans. I can't imagine that. President Wilson filed a formal protest. What would you have done if you were the President?

Later, this was one reason the United States joined World War One (the Great War). Do you think the Germans realized that might happen?

Next, a graphic organizer for response and evidence can help students arrange their thoughts.

Graphic Organizer for Response and Evidence

What happened with the Lusitania?	
What did the British do right?	What did the British do wrong?

Graphic Organizer for Response and Evidence	
What did the Germans do right?	What did the Germans do wrong?
Overall, who was right? Who was wrong? The British, the Germans, or both? Why (give specific examples)?	

Art (Grades 3 and Up)

> Create your own Jackson Pollock piece of art (https://jacksonpollock.org). Then, write a reflection explaining why your art is like Jackson Pollock's.

A graphic organizer can assist students as they process the task.

Art Reflection Graphic Organizer	
My Art	*Jackson Pollock's Art*
Why My Art is Like Jackson Pollock's.	

Upper Elementary Art

> Students move through an art gallery of work created by their classmates. Each student chooses one piece of art and writes a short critique. The critique must include the student's opinion of the artwork, support of the opinion based on the lesson taught by the teacher and the student's own experiences, and recommendations for improvement.

When writing a critique, it is helpful to model critiques, using examples and non-examples. Additionally, a graphic organizer can facilitate the evaluation process.

Art Evaluation Graphic Organizer	
What I think About the Art:	
What I Know About the Art from Class:	What I Know About the Art from My Life:
How to Improve:	

Technology (All Grades)

After our class online visit to the zoo, design a t-shirt about your trip. You'll need to use some of the following skills: save pictures you find online, cut and paste, image editing, inserting text, and image design. When you present your t-shirt to the class, justify your choices for the shirt based on your learning and your own experiences.

The technology activity incorporates multiple steps as students design a t-shirt. Because of the number of steps, a checklist is helpful.

Checklist for Designing a T-Shirt

- Search for pictures.
- Save pictures.
- Cut and paste into template.
- Edit as needed.
- Insert text as needed.

Additionally, a brainstorming graphic organizer can help students narrow down their choices.

Brainstorming About the Zoo

Everything I saw at the zoo:

My favorite part of the zoo:

What pictures I want to look for:

Physical Education (All Grades)

> For a specific physical education concept, such as throwing a ball, ask students to do the following:
>
> Demonstrate the skill twice for your partner (or the class). Ask your partner to identify whether you did the skill correctly or incorrectly. If correct, ask your partner to explain why it is correct. If incorrect, ask him or her to explain why it is not correct and then explain how to correct it.

Modeling is a foundational scaffold with this physical education activity. Students may need to visually how to demonstrate the skill, both correctly and incorrectly. Additionally, guiding questions as to what students see is helpful.

A Final Note

Scaffolding can encompass a wide range of strategies, including helping students learn to work together, participate in effective discourse, and activate their prior knowledge. We also need to model processes for students, use supportive questions without giving away the answer, and provide resources for students.

Points to Ponder

1. How will you use the information on students learning together and using discourse?
2. How might you improve your supportive questioning for students?
3. What resources do you need to provide for your students?
4. Which of the specific scaffolding strategies would you like to try?

Continue the Learning

Use the QR Code to access videos for your own use or for group professional development.

6

Assessment in the Productive Struggle Classroom

Once you have planned for productive struggle and implemented it, the natural question is how to assess it. We'll start by discussing the role of formative assessment, then move to discussing how to use formative assessment to measure the process of productive struggle and how to use summative assessment to measure the process.

Next, we'll turn our attention to options for using formative assessment to measure the content of productive struggle task, look at summative assessments to measure the content of productive struggle, and then talk about using rubrics to assess productive learning tasks.

Formative Assessment

Formative assessment is used periodically to check in with students and determine their understanding. It's designed for you to use it to inform your instruction and make appropriate adjustments, compared to summative assessment which provides summary information for grading. In this section, we'll be specifically addressing formative assessment for the process of productive struggle, and formative assessment for content.

Formative assessment, when used correctly, allows you to identify specific weaknesses for struggling students, and then gives you information on their progress. That's how you know what, how, and when to scaffold with your students. As you review the assessment strategies in this chapter, keep in mind the purpose is to improve your instruction and student learning. I prefer to use a teach-assess-then what flowchart.

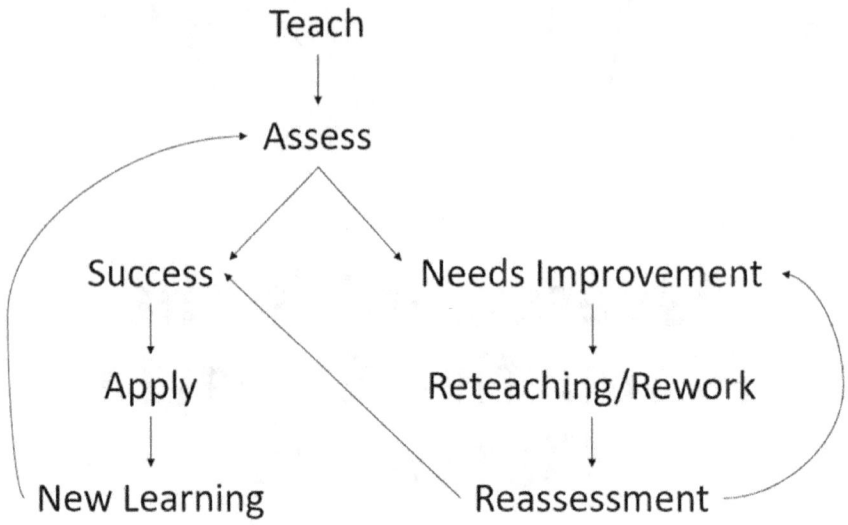

There are two broad ways to use formative assessment. First, you can assess individual student performance and use that information to help a particular student.

Forms for Formatively Assessing Individual Students

Individual Assessment	
Name	
What He/She Is Doing Well	What He/She Needs to Work On
What I Need To Do For This Student	

Class Roster			
Student	What They Are Doing Well	What They Need to Work On	Teacher's Next Step

Additionally, you can look at the overall picture of assessment for all students to understand patterns of performance. This can help you adjust your instruction for the class.

Patterns of Performance			
Use + if student mastered area, – if they are struggling, and 0 if they are totally stuck.			
Student's Name	Vocabulary	Understanding Connections	Facts and Content Mastery

Patterns of Performance			
Use + if student mastered area, – if they are struggling, and 0 if they are totally stuck.			
Student's Name	Vocabulary	Understanding Connections	Facts and Content Mastery

Pattern Analysis (review individual assessment to pull patterns)	
Pattern I Observed	My Next Steps

Assessing the Productive Struggle Process

Now let's look at a variety of engaging ways to assess the productive struggle process. You can easily adapt these to assess content if you prefer.

Observations

An important formative assessment tool for teachers is the use of observations. Observations can be planned, or they can be spontaneous. In an observation, you simply observe what students are doing, and take notes for documentation. You may choose to observe for productive struggle behaviors, or you may simply observe to see what happens from a general standpoint.

The most effective observations are planned. For example, if you want to see a student's problem-solving ability, you would schedule time to observe the student during the productive struggle task. The documentation, which may include simply taking notes, allows you to have a record of the student's skills at that point in time. By assessing it along with other formal and informal assessments, you gain a more accurate picture of the student's problem-solving abilities. You can also observe a student or a group. Also, it's important to note that during observations, you don't want to step in with a student. Rather, let them struggle and observe what is happening.

I've always found it helpful to use a template for observations.

Observation Template 1	
Student/Group	Date
Focus of Observation	
General Notes	
Strengths	Weaknesses
Next Steps	

This is a more structured alternative I've used in a group setting

Observation Template 2			
Group:			
	Strengths	*Challenges*	*Next Steps*
Sticking with the task when it isn't easy.			
Using graphic organizers and other tools when needed.			
Asking for help when needed.			

Checklists

Checklists are a strategy that can be used as a part of observations. Checklists can be simple yes/no tallies, or they can be open-ended for teachers to add notes.

Sample Mathematics Checklist	
Characteristic	*Notes*
Student demonstrates problem-solving ability.	
Student demonstrates persistence while solving problems.	
Student reflects on his/her thinking.	
Student shows applications of learning in real life.	

Sample Reading/Writing Checklist	
Characteristic	*Notes*
Student demonstrates persistence while writing.	
Student reflects throughout the process and uses metacognitive skills when appropriate.	
Student asks for help when needed, but only after struggling to solve problem himself/herself.	

Toolbox Check

A toolbox check can be used before students begin their productive struggle to assess if they have all their tools ready to use.

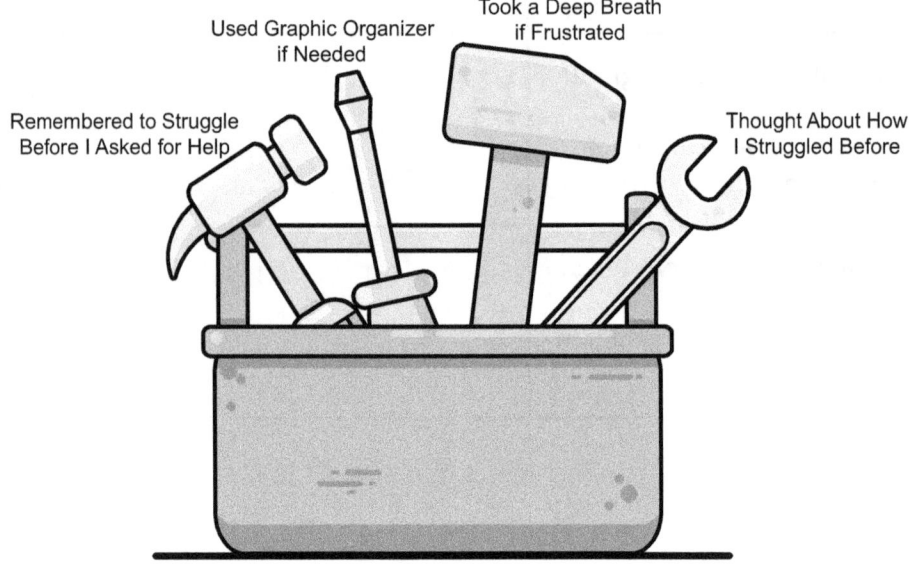

Mischievous Misconceptions

Throughout the productive struggle process, ask students to identify any misconceptions they have during the activity and what they learned that was correct. At the end, collect all the misconceptions and discuss them as a class.

Pause (paws) and Think

In this activity, students put up a "paw" on desk for the teacher to see, which means I'm pausing to think, check in on me.

I'm Pawsing

Stoplight

Another creative way is to use a stoplight to reflect their productive struggle process. Green means "I'm moving fine," yellow means "I'm struggling in a good way," and red means "I'm stuck."

Two Popsicles

Using this option, students are given a paper popsicle that is one color on side one, a different color on side two. Your school colors are one way to choose the colors. During the task or activity, you ask students to hold up their popsicle: One color means Struggling in a Good Way; the other color is Struggling in a Bad Way.

Stick to It

Each time they stick with a problem after a setback, they add a sticker to their path of footsteps.

Strategy Cards

Students are provided access to decks of strategy cards, cards that represent strategies they can use when they struggle. Samples include graphic organizers, drawing a picture, or asking what-if questions. Each time they use a strategy, they collect a card.

"I Sought Help" Cards

Students are provided access to decks of "I Sought Help" cards, cards that represent ways they can ask for help when they struggle. Samples include asked a friend or looked something up in a book or on the internet. Each time they use a strategy, they collect a card.

Rescue Request

Students draw or write to fill in a mini-comic strip showing "When I was stuck, I asked ___ for ___. Then...."

Rescue Request			
When I was stuck...	I asked...	For...	Then...

Weather Check-in

Part of productive struggle is how students feel while they are working. Using small cards, ask them to hold up a symbol that represents their feelings while working: sunny, cloudy, stormy, rainbow. Depending on their response, you may need to provide extra support, such as when they are stormy.

Summative Assessments for the Process of Productive Struggle

Now, let's look at strategies that you can do to assess the productive struggle process after they have completed the task or activity.

Checking My Toolbox Again

They can also revisit the toolbox after the activity to assess if or how they used the tools.

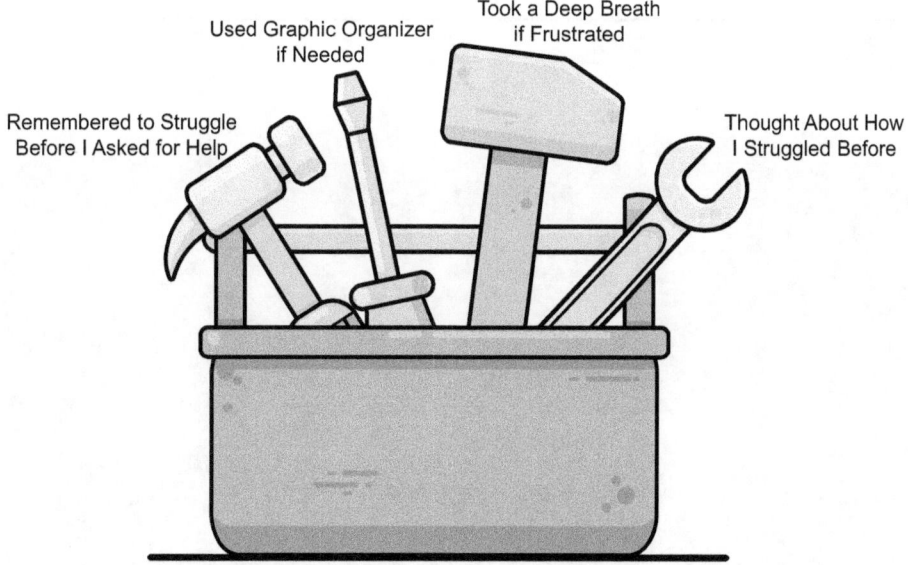

Sketch How You are Doing (Up, Great, Down, Not So Good, etc.)

Ask students to sketch the ups and downs of their activity, similar to a graph. They go up when they do well, down when it isn't as good, and in the middle if things are flat. Since they complete this during the activity, you can check in with students as a formative assessment, but discussing the finished form allows you to get a summative picture of the process. Students draw their own line to demonstrate how they are doing. For example, an up arrow means they are going up, a straight line means they are flat, etc.

When I Didn't Know What to Do

Another option is to do a certificate/feedback form for students to complete. They start with: "When I didn't know what to do...." and then complete "I did...."

When I Didn't Know What To Do . . .	
When I didn't know what to do . . .	Then I did . . .

Roses and Thorns

Another option is to use a rose metaphor. They identify thorns (things that stuck them) and then the flower is how they overcame them or succeeded.

Think Like a . . .

Ask students to reflect on the productive struggle task from the particular of a particular role related to the task. Then, they do a two minute video as to how they completed the task, using the chosen perspective.

> **"Think Like A" Roles**
> Author
> Writer
> Scientist
> Historian
> Mathematician

Stamina Thermometer

A great way to check in on the level of student persistence is the stamina thermometer.

Students color in sections of a thermometer icon to show how long they kept trying.

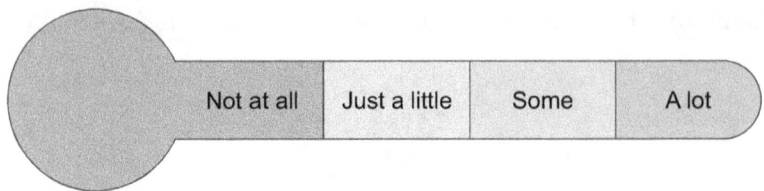

I'm Climbing Up

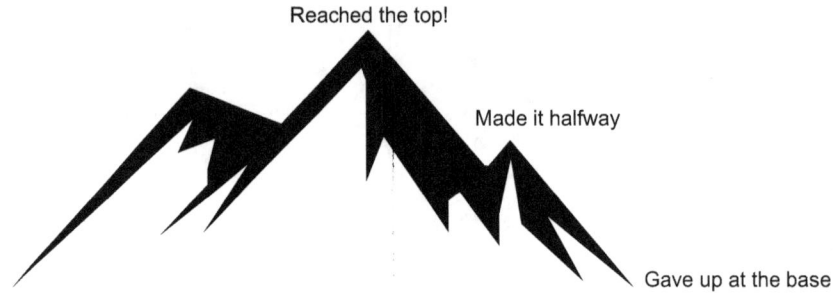

Helpfulness Badge

Complete/distribute badges for helpfulness. Both the asker and the helper earn a badge for help-seeking/giving.

Then I learned:
_____
_____

What Animal Am I?

Students choose the animal that represents their efforts for the activity.

Turtle	Penguin	Rabbit	Owl
Slow but steady	Waddled around	Kept running	Stayed calm and wise

Emoji Emotions

Students slide a clip or sticker along a range of emojis to reflect on how they managed their emotions while productively struggling.

Frustration Confused Thinking Okay Happy Excited

Checking In On Teamwork

We looked at this rubric in Chapter 3, but let's revisit it as a summative assessment. Students can use the rubric to self-assess, or you can use it to assess how well students worked in teams.

Collaborative Learning

	You're a Team Player 3	You're Working on It . . . 2	You're the Lone Ranger 1	Total for Each Category
G Group Dedication	I listened respectfully to my teammates' ideas and offered suggestions that helped my group.	I did listen to ideas, but I didn't give suggestions.	I was distracted and more interested in the other groups than my group.	**Group Dedication** I circled number 3 2 1
R Responsibility	I eagerly accepted responsibility with my group and tried to do my part to help everyone in my group.	I accepted responsibility within my group without arguing.	I quarreled and did not accept roles given by my group.	**Responsibility** I circled number 3 2 1
O Open Communication	I listened to others' ideas and tried to solve conflicts peacefully.	I listened to others' ideas, but did not try to solve conflicts.	I was controlling and argumentative to my group.	**Open Communication** I circled number 3 2 1

Collaborative Learning

	You're a Team Player 3	You're Working on It . . . 2	You're the Lone Ranger 1	Total for Each Category
U **Use of Work Time**	I was involved and engaged; I encouraged my group the entire time we were working.	I tried my best the entire time we were working.	I was not involved and did not offer any suggestions for the good of the group.	**Use of Work Time** I circled number 3 2 1
P **Participation**	I was a team member. I offered ideas, suggestions, and help for my group.	I participated in the project, but did not offer to help anyone.	I did not participate because I was not interested.	**Participation** I circled number 3 2 1
				Total _____

Overall Summary of Productive Struggle

If you want an overall picture of their productive struggle from the student's standpoint, you might use a formal self-assessment.

Self-Assessment of Productive Struggle Activity

I feel good about what I did today.	☺	☹
If I was struggling, I continued to try.	☺	☹
If I got stuck, I tried some different ways.	☺	☹
If I tried and was still stuck, I asked for help.	☺	☹
If I got stuck, I thought about what I've done other times.	☺	☹
I tried to use things that help me, such as graphic organizers.	☺	☹

Self-Assessment of Productive Struggle Activity Upper Elementary			
	Yes	No	Why?
I feel good about what I did today.			
If I was struggling, I continued to try.			
If I got stuck, I tried some different ways.			
If I tried and was still stuck, I asked for help.			

Self-Assessment of Productive Struggle Activity Upper Elementary				
	Yes	No	Why?
If I got stuck, I thought about what I've done other times.			
I tried to use things that help me, such as graphic organizers.			

Beginner's Rubric for Productive Struggle

Finally, you can use the rubric below to assess individual students, assess groups of students, or allow them to self-assess progress for themselves or their group, using the five dispositions from Chapter 2.

Student Dispositions Rubric			
Category	*Beginning*	*Developing*	*Proficient*
Curiosity	Shows little interest in something new or asking questions.	When prompted, student asks questions or shows interest in something new.	Regularly asks thoughtful questions and often explores new ideas.
Persistence	Quits when student isn't successful.	Is willing to try again if teacher encourages him or her.	Doesn't give up on the first try and regularly tries again.
Problem-Solving	Struggles with complex problems and typically only tries one strategy.	With guidance, student will struggle to solve complex problems and try alternatives.	Student works independently to solve complex problems and will try alternatives.

	Student Dispositions Rubric		
Category	*Beginning*	*Developing*	*Proficient*
Taking Risks	Student works on easy tasks and does not like to try new things.	With guidance, student tries new things. With encouragement, will try again after making mistake.	Student tries challenging tasks independently and works through mistakes.
Making Connections	Does not connect learning to real life or other subjects.	Makes some connections to other subjects or real life.	Regularly connects ideas across subjects and to real-life experiences.

Now, let's turn our attention to formative and summative strategies for assessing the content during the productive struggle process.

Formatively Assessing the Content During the Process

Build-a-Billboard

At some point during the learning, ask students to stop and build a billboard. Students take a piece of paper and create a quick billboard showing what they have learned.

Illustrate Connections

Ask students to draw the connections they have made during the lesson so far.

Around the Circle (Each Person Says One Thing, Keep Going)

If students are working in groups, go around in a circle and ask each person to say one thing they have learned and one question they still have.

What's the Big Picture?

Ask students to share "the big picture." In other words, they share a real-life connection they have made during their learning.

Explain It to Someone

Pretend you are a famous person or character related to the task. Ask students to explain what they are learning to your person/character.

SOS

Students write or draw a quick summary, their opinion about what they have learned, and support or evidence for their opinion.

Word Cloud Generator

Ask students to use vocabulary from their task to create a word cloud. They can do this manually or with a free online tool.

Pipe Cleaner/Craft Stick

Students use a fuzzy craft stick to create a shape that represents their learning. Then, they explain why the shape demonstrates their learning.

Bumper Sticker Summary

Students create a bumper sticker with images and words that summarizes their learning.

Make It New

Make it New allows you to see if students can apply their learning. Students choose an image: a book, a face, the earth, or an exclamation point.

Then, they write how what they have learned applies to another book/text they have read, themselves, the real world, or something else.

Make it New			
How it applies to another book/text	*How it applies to me*	*How it applies to the real world*	*How it applies to something else*

You've Got Mail

In one of their blogs, Edutopia (www.edutopia.org/resource/checking-understanding-download) recommends using "You've Got Mail." As the author describes it,

> Each student writes a question about a topic on the front of an envelope; the answer is included inside. Questions are then "mailed" around the room. Each learner writes his or her answer on a slip of scratch paper and confirms its correctness by reading the "official answer" before placing his or her own response in the envelope. After several series of mailings and a class discussion about the subject, the envelopes are deposited in the teacher's letterbox.

Wall of Knowledge

Angela Stockman, on the blog brilliant-insane.com, describes "Add a Brick to the Wall of Knowledge." She recommends creating a bulletin board, and giving students paper bricks. Ask them to write about what they have learned, and place (or staple) their bricks on the wall throughout the year. You could also give students boxes, and they could write new learning on the different sides of the box. Stack the boxes together to create a wall.

Bounce the Ball

In Bounce the Ball, use a beach ball to assess what students know. The first student makes a point about the lesson. Then, they throw the ball to another student who either expands on the first point, asks a question, or makes another point. The game continues until students run out of points.

Always-Sometimes-Never True

In Always-Sometimes-Never True, the teacher makes a statement that could meet any of the three options. Then, students move to the front, middle, or back of the room to discuss their choice. Finally, the teacher leads a whole-group discussion. This is particularly helpful when there is not a yes or no choice.

Summative Assessment of the Content

To summatively assess the content of the productive struggle lesson, you want to focus on two characteristics.

> Accurately measures what the students learned.
> Decide the level of struggle for the assessment.

First, be sure the type of summative assessment accurately measures what the students learned. For example, if students created a project, the project itself can be the summative assessment. However, you may also want to use a short answer or essay question so that students can reflect of their learning. Alternatively, should you want to measure knowledge of facts, true-false, matching, or multiple choice tests may be appropriate.

Next, decide if you want an element of struggle in the summative assessment or if you want it to be written at an easier level. Realistically, that is up to you. I prefer to still have a level of challenge in my assessments, but you may not want that. I'll be giving you options for more challenge should you want to use them.

Traditional Types of Summative Assessment

Matching Tests
True-False Tests
Multiple-Choice Tests
Short Answers
Essay Questions

Matching Tests

Matching tests are an easy, quick way to assess a wide range of student knowledge. However, it is difficult to assess at a higher level of challenge, as most matching tests measure basic recall questions. Depending on the items, students can guess rather than truly demonstrate understanding.

What are the best strategies for developing quality matching tests? First, make sure there is one best option for each item you list. Ensure that students can see why the items match so there is clear evidence students understand the link. Also, provide more examples than matching items. For example, if you have a list of vocabulary terms and then definitions, add one or two extra definitions to increase the challenge.

Another option to increase challenge is to use a three-column matching test. With this choice, students must understand three levels of content rather than two.

Headings for Three-column Matching Test		
Shape	*Description*	*Example*

True-False Tests

True-false tests are an excellent way for students to determine the accuracy of a statement, agree with opinions, and define terms. As with matching items, they are graded quickly and easily, and students can answer a wide range of questions in a short amount of time. However, once again, questions are typically low-level recall questions, and you may not be sure students understand the question or if they are simply guessing. To combat this and to increase the challenge, require students to rewrite any false choices as true statements, which does require them to demonstrate a true understanding of the content.

Multiple-Choice Tests

Multiple-choice tests are probably the most commonly used tests in classrooms across the nation, and they have several benefits. Although due in part to preparation for standardized tests, they are also easy to score. They also apply to a wide range of cognitive skills, including higher-order-thinking ones. Finally, incorrect answers, if written and explained correctly, can help you diagnose a student's problem areas. Disadvantages include that the questions can't measure a student's ability to create or synthesize information and that students can guess an answer.

There are three ways to write multiple-choice questions that allow you to increase the challenge. First, choose a question that moves beyond basic recall. Next, create choices for the stem that are clearly correct or incorrect without making them too easy. In other words, if we provide examples that are clearly off topic, it makes it easier for students to guess. Finally, although some teachers do not like to use "all of the above," "none of the above," "a and d" options, or "mark all of the above," we do find they require students to think at a higher level than basic recall. Remember, you know your students; adapt the suggestions so they match your students' needs.

Short-Answer Questions

Short-answer questions are an expanded form of fill-in-the-blank. Responses are not as long as essays, but they usually include more than one sentence. Because students are required to create a response, they are more challenging than the types of items we've already discussed. You'll need to build challenge into the context of your questions, asking questions that require more than just a list. Although more challenging to grade than matching, true-false, fill-in-the-blank and multiple-choice questions, they are simpler than assessing essay questions.

Essay Questions

Essay questions are one of the most common assessments used in today's classrooms. Essay questions are extremely effective for measuring complex learning. Opportunities for guessing are removed, so you can truly measure what students understand. There are several disadvantages, including the amount of time to grade them, the subjective nature of grading and the dependency of the answer on the student's writing ability.

When you are writing essay questions, crafting the question is particularly important. You want to be sure the complexity of the learning outcome is reflected in a clear, focused manner. It's also important to provide explicit instructions as to your expectations.

> Explain what you wanted to discover with your investigation. How did your investigation answer the question? Provide evidence from your investigation to support your opinion.

Performance-Based Assessment

Performance-based assessments are a type of summative assessments, but they differ from traditional testing. They are focused on students performing in some manner to demonstrate their understanding. Typically, performance-based assessments are more challenging, because students must go in depth to complete the performance, project, or portfolio. Many of the productive struggle tasks and activities provided throughout the book were examples of performance-based assessments.

Using Rubrics for Summative Assessment

Particularly when using performance-based tasks and assessments, rubrics are helpful. They assist students in understanding the task, and they help teachers with grading.

How do you develop a rubric? First, decide on the categories that you will be assessing, as well as a scale for scoring. Then, write the indicators for each category and score. I'd add a caution here—too often, we base our scoring on quantity (includes 1 reason vs. 3 reasons) when we really want quality. Keep that in mind with your descriptors. Finally, share the rubric with your students and gather feedback. This way you can ensure the rubric accurately measures what you want. You can even create it together with your students. Here's a sample you can use when students are presenting information.

Rubric for Speaking

	Not Enough ☹	Too Much ☹	Just Right ☺
S Stay on topic	We're not sure what you are talking about	You're talking about so much; we can't pick out what is important.	We understand your topic and your most important points.
P Pick your volume	We can't hear you.	You don't need to shout!	Perfect volume: loud for whole group; soft for partner; medium for small group.
E Eye contact	You're looking down.	You're looking at everything but us!	You are looking at your audience throughout your talk.
A Audience	What you are saying is too easy for us; we know it already.	What you are saying is too hard; we don't understand.	Great! It's not too easy, and not too hard.
K Know your stuff	You look very nervous.	You're acting like a know-it-all.	We felt like you were talking with us and helping us understand.

Now, let's go back to one of our examples from earlier in the book.

> Ask students to write a persuasive letter to the principal, asking him or her to change a school rule they want to change. In addition to stating their position, they should provide specific reasons for the change as well as real-life examples for each reason.

Here's a sample rubric to use with students.

Sample Rubric			
	Starting	*Working On It*	*This Is Great!*
Persuasion	An opinion is simply stated, but not in a persuasive manner.	There are some persuasive elements in the letter.	Persuasion is woven into every part of the letter.
Reasons for Change	Reasons for the change are not stated or are vague.	Reasons for change are clearly stated.	Reasons for the change are clearly stated and are linked to the opinion.
Real-Life Examples	Real-life examples are not included or are not appropriate.	Examples are real life and support the opinion.	Multiple real-life examples thoroughly support the opinion.

Online sources such as Rubistar and iRubric, as well as many AI tools, can help you build rubrics. It's also worth a Google search to see if there is an existing rubric you might use or adapt.

A Final Note

Formative assessment for both the process and content of productive struggle can assist with improving instruction. It can also support your scaffolding. Additionally, it's important to use summative assessment for how students do productive struggle (the process) and the content of the productive struggle task. Using a variety of strategies for both formative and summative assessment will ensure you can positively impact student learning.

Points to Ponder

1. What formative process strategy would you like to try?
2. What formative product strategy would you like to try?
3. What summative process strategy would you like to try?
4. What summative product strategy would you like to try?

Continue the Learning

Use the QR Code to access videos for your own use or for group professional development.

7

Common Concerns About Productive Struggle

In this chapter, I'd like to address four questions that teachers commonly ask me about productive struggle.

> How should I address productive struggle with students with special needs?
>
> How do I address students who won't try?
>
> How do I communicate with parents and families about productive struggle?
>
> It seems to take a lot of time to plan and implement productive struggle in my classroom. I'm overwhelmed. What can I do?

How Should I Address Productive Struggle With Students With Special Needs?

This is a critical issue with productive struggle. When determining and using activities for students with special needs, the first consideration is the IEP. The *Individualized Education Plan* is a legal document that ensures students' specialized needs are met. It specifies any accommodations and/or modifications you must provide to a student. In our book, *Rigor for Students with Special Needs, 2nd edition,* Brad Witzel and I provided an overview of modifications and accommodations.

Accommodations

Accommodations are changes that can be made to the way students with disabilities are instructed and assessed. The changes can be made to instructional methods and materials, assignments and assessments, learning environment, time demands and schedules, and/or special communication systems.

When deciding on the appropriate accommodation, consider the following questions:

Student Accommodation Consideration			
Step	Consideration	Question	Response per Student
1	Access	Does the student have an impairment that restricts access to the skill being assigned or tested?	
2	Availability	What accommodations (if any) are aligned with the impairment and available to provide access?	
3	Target	Will the accommodation maintain the construct being assigned or tested?	

Source: adapted from Kettler, (2012)

Modifications

Modifications are changes to what a student is expected to learn. In other words, the standard or concept is changed from general education expectations. Content modifications likely change what the test measures (McDonnell, McLaughlin, & Morison, 1997). Modifications, for example, may include deleting certain items that are inappropriate for an examinee or making constructed-response questions into multiple-choice questions. These types of modifications are presumed to change the nature of what is being tested. For standardized assessments, safeguards exist to secure that the construct of the question will not be altered or modified. Thus, the more modifications given to a student during their learning, the less likely that they will be prepared for an unmodified assessment.

Sample Accommodations and Modifications

Your state and/or school district may have an approved list of accommodations and modifications, but here are a few of the most common ones.

Sample Accommodations and Modifications	
Potential Accommodations	*Potential Modifications*
Presentation ♦ Written directions, rather than only oral ♦ Written or guided notes to go with lecture ♦ Chunked lesson in small increments ♦ Increased volume ♦ Increased text size	Assessment ♦ Different content ♦ Different questions ♦ Different responses required ♦ Excuse from the assessment ♦ Tools to answer standards-focused questions (e.g. dictionary for vocabulary or calculator for computational fluency)
Response ♦ Dictation software for written assignments ♦ Shortened assignments with same content ♦ Spellcheck or dictionary, unless vocabulary/spelling objective ♦ Chunked assignment in smaller increments	Assignment ♦ Different project ♦ Eliminated part of a project ♦ Different questions ♦ Eliminated questions ♦ Different responses required ♦ Tools to answer standards-focused questions (i.e. dictionary for vocabulary or calculator for computational fluency)
Timing ♦ Increased time to complete test or assignment ♦ Increased wait time ♦ Frequent breaks/chunked assignment or test	Curriculum ♦ Different or eliminated standards ♦ Different grading

| **Sample Accommodations and Modifications** ||
Potential Accommodations	*Potential Modifications*
Setting ♦ Reduced distraction environment ♦ Use of sensory tool for attention and focus ♦ Preferable seating location ♦ Different lighting	
Scheduling ♦ Increased time to move between classes ♦ Tests given a specific time of the day	
Organization ♦ Visual timer and scheduler ♦ Use of a planner, checked by teachers ♦ More frequent assignment reminders ♦ Additional assignment clarification ♦ Weekly progress report	

Source: adapted from https://www.understood.org/en/learning-thinking-differences/treatments-approaches/educational-strategies/common-classroom-accommodations-and-modifications

The IEP is only the first step. You'll also want to consider what you know about the student in order to best meet his or her needs. Think of it this way—the IEP is the floor, not the ceiling. Use it to ensure success, but don't let it limit a student. I've found charting out information to be helpful when planning and using my assessments.

Assessment Form	
Based on the IEP and/or my pre-assessment data, what do I need to do with this student?	
My formative assessment plan	Modifications and accommodations needed based on the formative assessment
Summative assessment	Modifications and accommodations in the summative assessment

How Do I Address Students Who Won't Try?

Repeated failures and low achievement associated with learning disabilities often lead students to attribute their failures to internal causes and successes to external causes such as luck or ease of the task (Dweck & Elliott, 1983; Settle & Milich, 1999). When this is repeated over years, students develop a learned helplessness, knowing that they will fail, despite even good scores on tests and assignments. Therefore, it is fair to conclude that students with a history of academic failure develop learned helplessness.

Learned helplessness is a process of conditioning where student seek help from others even when they have mastered information. See if this example looks familiar:

> A student is asked to solve a direct reading comprehension problem, but he immediately raises his hand. When the teacher comes over, the student says he needs help. So the teacher reads the paragraph to the student and re-explains the question. The student still doesn't answer the question. Next, the teacher re-explains a regularly used comprehension strategy with the student. Finally, the teacher walks through the strategy and may even solve the problem for the student.

While this scenario sounds justifiable, and maybe even familiar, the teacher is reinforcing the student's learned helplessness. This exchange undermines the student's independent ability to solve the problem. Such exchanges that continue a student's learned helplessness include an increased time of completion, lack of academic perseverance, refusal to initiate an attempt, or general off-task behavior. Thus, once a student has begun a run of learned helplessness, expect to see the outcomes repeatedly. In the previous scenario, the student must learn to attend to the teacher's group instruction and attempt to solve problems.

Instead of running to the rescue of students who can succeed without us or even refuse to help such students, it is important to find ways to teach students to gain independence in their problem-solving. In other words, find out why the student is behaving in a certain way and plan a response that best builds academic success and independence. One way to help is to teach students how to learn and succeed without instantly making excuses and asking for help by following these steps.

1. Determine if learned helplessness exists
2. Explicitly model the student the preferred academic behavior
3. Teach the student a strategy for displaying the preferred academic behavior
4. Provide practice for the strategy
5. Set a cue to remind the student to initiate the strategy
6. Allow the student to succeed
7. Facilitate the student's problem solving strategy

There are other strategies that can help with learned helplessness. These include normalizing mistakes so they are more willing to try, reframing mistakes so students see them as opportunities, setting achievable goals so they do not see the task as overwhelming, and providing choice when possible.

How Do I Communicate With Parents and Families About Productive Struggle?

There are three ways to communicate with parents and families.

> Communication to Parents and Families
> Communication from Parents and Families
> Communication with Parents and Families

Communication to Parents and Families

When I talk to parents, many of them feel as though there is a hidden code in schools; a code they don't understand. Margo and her son moved to a new area when Jared started school. She missed the first parent-teacher meeting because she was working. She called the school and left several messages asking to meet with his teacher but didn't receive a return call. Margo was frustrated when she told me her story. Another teacher at the school was in one of my classes, so I talked with her. I discovered that the school had a policy that all appointments with teachers were scheduled with the attendance secretary. My graduate student said the principal always explained the policy at the first meeting. So, of course, Margo didn't know because she wasn't at the meeting, and she thought the teacher was just ignoring her. One phone call later, she connected with the teacher, and she and Jared finished the year successfully.

I recommend you have a one page fact sheet about productive struggle in your classroom. By clearly describing what you are doing, parents are more likely to understand what is happening. In addition to making it accessible to parents and families through your website, remind families of critical aspects through social media postings and newsletters.

Productive Struggle
One Page Fact Sheet

What Is Productive Struggle?

Productive struggle is the process of students grappling with a challenging task, making mistakes, and continuing to persist in order to build deeper learning.

Why are We Using Productive Struggle?

We want all our students to learn at higher levels rather than just doing easy work. We want them to use problem-solving skills and learn life skills such as persistence and independence.

Important Facts:

- When students work at levels that do not require struggle, they do not necessarily make progress.
- Learning to persist through struggle is a life skill for students and also helps them become more independent and confident learners.
- When students struggle and continue to learn, they learn at higher levels.

What You'll See With Your Student

There will be times he or she will asked to work individually or in groups on tasks that are challenging. These will be tasks that are not too easy and not impossible, but they are ones your son or daughter will find challenging. Ahead of time, teachers will model what students are expected to do, and they will teach students ways to help themselves during the activity. Teachers are also available for help, but will encourage students to try themselves before they ask for help.

What You Can Do

When your son or daughter is struggling, encourage him or her to continue to work, and to use the strategies the teacher has provided. Don't do the work for them—that's the worst thing you can do. Ask lots of questions that can help your student, such as "How have you handled this before?" or "How can you figure this out on your own?"

For More Information

Contact your student's teacher for more assistance.

I spoke with one teacher about providing information to families. A parent asked her about how she could support her son when he was struggling. She had a simple response.

> A part of productive struggle is grit, which is sticking with something important to you even when it's hard, boring, or takes time according to Angela Duckworth. Grit is important because it can help predict long term success and it helps develop resilience. As your student is working with productive struggle, you can encourage grit by modeling your own perseverance, praise effort, not just results, and remind them that failure is a part of learning.

Keeping it simple, yet clear is helpful. Additionally, whenever students are working on a productive struggle project, make those expectations clear not only to students, but to parents in writing. One of my principals always reminded me, "The worst thing you can hear from a parent is 'If I had only known.'" Your goal is no surprises!

Communication From Parents and Families

It's also important to have communication from parents and families. There will be times that you need information from them in order to best meet the needs of your students. I remember talking to a neighbor a few years ago. She had received multiple calls and emails from the school, but had not returned them. She was worried they wanted to give her bad news. I convinced her to call her son's teacher. The teacher was simply concerned because her son's performance was deteriorating. The teacher wanted to help, but wondered if anything was happening at home. My neighbor explained that her ex-husband was remarrying, and her son was unsure as to what that would mean to him. The teacher was empathetic, and assured my neighbor she would provide extra help at school to ensure his success. My neighbor was relieved to know of the additional support, and the teacher was able to provide that support since she knew the situation.

I like to periodically ask parents and family members for key information.

Feedback Form	
How do you think your son/daughter is doing in school?	
Is there anything you are concerned about?	

Feedback Form	
What can I do to help your son/daughter?	
Is there anything else I should know?	

Communication With Parents and Families

Finally, there is communication with parents and families. This is the highest level of communication, representing a true back-and-forth in which, together, you make decisions about a student.

There are 10 keys to effective communication that are helpful.

> **10 Principles of Effective Communication**
>
> Conciseness and consistency matter
> Open with your key point
> Match to your agenda
> Make it coherent
> Understand your audience
> Name your objective/desired action
> Courtesy rules
> Ask questions
> Tell a story
> Empathy helps

Using these keys can help you develop a true partnership. Although you'll want to consider them anytime you are communicating, they are especially helpful during conferences. Keep these in mind as you review my five steps for a GREAT parent/family conference.

> Good news is the way to start!
> Relate your opinion so they understand you want to help their child.
> Evidence is provided to support your opinion.
> Accept their perspective as valid.
> Thought-provoking questions help all participants share.

It's our responsibility to connect with parents and families; and the benefits outweigh any costs in terms of time.

It Seems to Take a Lot of Time to Plan and Implement Productive Struggle in My Classroom. I'm Overwhelmed. What Can I Do?

Managing all aspects of productive struggle can be overwhelming. Staying organized is a key aspect of using productive struggle effectively. I've found there are 3 key strategies that can help.

> Streamline the Process
> Organize Your Files
> Collect Your Key Resources

Streamline the Process

First, streamline what you do. You want to be effective, but you don't want to have so many choices that it overwhelms you. For example, I visited a kindergarten teacher one day. She regularly used K-W-Ls for pre-assessment, which is a great tool. However, she opened a file drawer and showed me almost 200 patterns for K-W-Ls—one for each day of the year. That's great—but you don't need that. If you want some variety in the look of a graphic organizer, have a few, but don't go overboard.

In another situation, a teacher shared with me her coding for feedback on student work. She had been writing out every comment on every paper. She realized that, for the most part, she used 7–10 general comments. She developed a code for those, taught it to students and families, and was able to save about 60% of her grading time by using the code. She could then focus on comments at the end or in a unique situation.

Organize Your Files

Another important aspect of managing assessment is to organize your files. You can do this with paper or electronically. Start with the basics. Build a folder for general pre-assessments, one for productive struggle formative assessments, then one for productive struggle summative assessments. You'll put generic options here that you can pull for use at any time.

Next, move to specific subjects if you teach more than one. Build similar folders that work just for that content area. Third, and this is most critical, build folders for each unit or topic you teach and organize the tasks, formative assessments, and summative assessments. This is your go-to set of folders next year when you are teaching the same topic. Don't be overwhelmed with this—just organize as you go through the year, and then you'll have it done. Again, it's up to you whether you organize with paper or electronically. Choose what works best for you.

Collect Your Key Resources

Finally, you probably have some key productive struggle resources that you regularly access. It's time to organize those too! I use two electronic methods for this, but you can also do it with printouts. First, I bookmark all my key resources in a folder called productive struggle. If you want to be super organized, you can have subfolders here for rubrics, tasks, graphic organizers, etc.

I also keep an email folder for productive struggle. These are emails I receive that contain resources I want to review later. When I have time, I read the information and bookmark as necessary.

A Final Note

When incorporating productive struggle in your classroom, you may face particular challenges. Addressing students with special needs, working with those who won't try, communicating with parents, and finding time to plan are important issues to deal with.

Points to Ponder

1. What strategy can help you work with students with special needs?
2. How can you address learned helplessness in your situation?
3. How would you like to communicate with parents about productive struggle?
4. What tip on finding and managing time would you like to try?

Continue the Learning

Use the QR Code to access videos for your own use or for group professional development.

8

Collaborating for Productive Struggle

One of the things we have learned as educators is that working together makes us more effective. This is particularly true when we are trying to improve our instruction in productive struggle. Many teachers are members of professional learning communities.

The original meaning of a professional community of learners reflected the commitment of teachers and leaders who continuously seek to grow professionally and act upon their new learning. Learning communities are focused on student learning. Teachers who belong to a learning community want to improve their classroom instruction. In this chapter, we'll focus on three areas related to collaboration and learning communities.

> How Can I Find Time to Work With Other Teachers?
> What Does Collaboration Look Like?
> Activities for Professional Learning Communities

How Can I Find Time to Work With Other Teachers?

It is important that teachers have time to work with colleagues on professional tasks. This collaborative time is one of the catalysts for nurturing and sustaining change. Teachers value the opportunity to meet with grade or content peers to discuss successes, diagnose ways to improve, develop a repertoire of strategies that they can use in their own classrooms, and provide critical input to school improvement plans.

There are many different ways to provide collaborative time and they vary considerably depending on the grade level of the school. Unfortunately, most of these options are not controlled by teachers. I share them so that you can consider options to discuss with your leadership team. These samples are from Ronald Williamson in our leadership book, *7 Strategies for School Improvement*.

Ways to Provide Collaborative Time	
Common Planning	When teachers share a common planning period some of the time may be used for collaborative work.
Parallel Scheduling	When special teachers (physical education, music, art, etc.) are scheduled so that grade level or content area teachers have common planning.
Shared Classes	Teachers in more than one grade or team combine their students into a single large class for specific instruction and the other teachers can collaborate.
Faculty Meeting	Find other ways to communicate the routine items shared during faculty meetings and reallocate that time to collaborative activities.
Adjust Start or End of Day	Members of a team, grade, or entire school agree to start their workday early or extend their workday one day a week to gain collaborative time.
Late Start or Early Release	Adjust the start or end of the school day for students and use the time for collaborative activity.
Professional Development Days	Rather than traditional large group professional development use the time for teams of teachers to engage in collaborative work.

Angela Evans, the Instructional Dean at Tulsa Technology Center shared how her school provides collaborative time. They developed a "released time" schedule that allows every teacher to work with other teachers on instructional issues. The deans organize the schedule to provide two days during the year for this important work.

Regardless of the way you provide time for collaboration, the most important thing is how the time is used. It is important that it be productive and supports your school's vision, and only the participants can control that.

What Does Collaboration Look Like?

In *The Essential Guide to Professional Learning: Collaboration*, the Australian Institute for Teaching and School Leadership points out there is an important difference between collaboration, which is the goal of Professional Learning Communities, and cooperation.

Collaboration vs. Cooperation	
Collaboration "to work with another or others on a joint project"	*Cooperation* "to be of assistance or willing to help"
Joint planning, decision-making, and problem-solving Job embedded and long term Formal and informal Common goals High levels of trust	Individual ownership of goals with others providing assistance for mutual benefit Resources and materials are shared as required Often spontaneous arrangements Passive engagement by others Often short term No set structure or arrangements

Notice the differences between the two. It's a bit like putting two pens beside each other vs. using a pen with four colors inside it. Do you truly work together?

Activities for Professional Learning Communities

Although there are many ways for teachers to work together, we are going to take a look at 7 of the most common.

> **Seven Activities for Professional Learning Communities**
>
> A Parade of Productive Struggle: Sharing My Lesson
>
> Playback for Progress: Video Observations of Productive Struggle
>
> Peeking with Purpose: Visiting Classrooms to see Productive Struggle
>
> "I Spy" for Patterns with Productive Struggle
>
> Learning in Action Through Lesson Studies
>
> Looking at the How: Developing Consistent Expectations for the Process of Productive Struggle
>
> Looking at Student Work: Developing Consistent Expectations for the Products of Productive Struggle

A Parade of Productive Struggle: Sharing My Lesson

One way you can work together as a small or large group of teachers is to have a Lesson Plan Parade. Ask each teacher to share a lesson plan with productive struggle and post it on the wall around the room. Teachers "read the room" and post ribbons with a positive statement about each lesson plan. This works well as a springboard for planning additional productive struggle lessons.

Playback for Progress: Video Observations of Productive Struggle

Another option to improve your productive struggle instruction is to watch other lessons. You may find some online, or teachers can take turns videoing a lesson in their class. What's key is looking at all aspects of the lesson.

Video Viewing Guide	
Productive Struggle Focus	
What Happened Before Productive Struggle to Enhance Student Success	
Instruction for the Process	Instruction for the Content
What I Noticed During Productive Struggle	
About the Process	About the Content
What I Noticed After the Productive Struggle	
Successes I Want to Share	Challenges I Want to Discuss

Over time, you will begin to notice patterns you see in multiple lessons, which can help everyone improve their instruction.

Peeking With Purpose: Visiting Classrooms to See Productive Struggle

If you are able to physically visit classrooms, that is an ideal way to learn about productive struggle. I've found at the elementary school level, it works well to visit other grade levels, since teachers at the same grade level typically have planning at the same time. Ideally, you can discuss the lesson with the teacher to be observed in advance and receive a lesson plan or outline so you know what you will be seeing. You can use the video guide from earlier, or the alternate provided next.

Peeking With Purpose Observation Form	
Lesson focus:	
How productive struggle will be implemented in the lesson:	
What I noticed about students doing the work (persistence, etc.)	What I noticed about the task

"I Spy" for Patterns With Productive Struggle

Learning walks provide a "snapshot" of what is happening in classrooms. They are not used for evaluative purposes or for individual feedback; rather, their purpose is to help teachers learn about overall instruction. Additionally, the goal is to identify areas of instructional strengths, as well as possible challenges. You are also not watching a full lesson, but are visiting for about 10 minutes. Since you are dropping in and out of classrooms, you are looking for overall patterns within a grade level, subject area, or school. You may also want to begin with looking for positive examples, in order to build trust.

"I Spy" Pattern Notes		
	Positive Points	*Questions I Have*
Classroom One		
Classroom Two		
Classroom Three		
Patterns I Noticed		

A school in Chicago organized "I Spy" days. Teachers dropped in on classrooms for 5–10 minutes in order to identify positive examples of instruction. Teachers came back together after school with their "detective notebooks" to share what they had seen. It was an invigorating experience for teachers, who said this was the first time they had a chance to look at other classrooms. As one teacher explained, "I don't get time to visit other teachers' classes. I learned so much, and I have two new ideas I want to implement tomorrow."

Learning in Action Through Lesson Studies

Lesson studies emphasize working in small groups to plan, teach, observe, and critique a lesson. It's an excellent reflection of the principles of professional learning communities, as the goal is to systematically examine your teaching in order to become more effective.

In a lesson study, teachers work together to develop a detailed plan for a lesson. One member of the group teaches the lesson to his or her students, while other members of the group observe. Next, the group discusses their observations about the lesson and student learning.

Teachers revise the lesson based on their observations, then a second group member teaches the lesson, with other members once again observing. Then, the group meets to discuss the revised lesson. Finally, teachers talk about what the study lesson taught them and how they can apply the learning in their own classroom.

Steps in a Lesson Study

Teachers choose a lesson focus.

Teachers develop the lesson, which includes productive struggle.

One teacher teaches the lesson.

Other teachers observe the lesson, either live or on video.

Teachers discuss what they observed.

Teachers revise the lesson.

Second teacher teachers the lesson.

Other teachers observe the lesson, either live or on video.

Teacher discuss the revised lesson.

Teachers discuss what the lesson and process taught them and how they can apply the learning.

Looking at the How: Developing Consistent Expectations for the Process of Productive Struggle

It's important to have consistent expectations within a grade level, and across grade levels. Ideally, for the process of productive struggle—what productive struggle looks like and how students approach it—you want to be consistent across all teachers in your school. It may look a bit different in kindergarten and fifth grade, but there are basic expectations that should be consistent. Here's my recommended process for developing consistent expectations on the "how" of productive struggle.

Research productive struggle through books, articles, and videos.

Teachers share ideas as to what productive struggle looks like (persistence, only asking for help after trying on your own first, etc.). Take all ideas and chart them out.

Organize the ideas by patterns or categories (help seeking, using scaffolding tools, etc.).

Reword words and phrases to be student friendly.

Create a chart students can follow.

Implement the chart.

Teachers make necessary adjustments as needed.

Sample Student Chart of Productive Struggle Expectations

☺	☹
Try it yourself first.	Immediately ask the teacher for help.
If it's hard, keep trying!	Give up before you start.

Looking at Student Work: Developing Consistent Expectations for the Products of Productive Struggle

A final way to improve productive struggle is to look at authentic student work. When you examine and evaluate student work, you can clarify your own standards for work, strengthen common expectations for students, or align curriculum across classrooms.

It's important that the discussion is focused on results, not on personalities. At the beginning of the process, agree on a process for the discussion. Templates are also helpful to keep everyone on the same page.

Discuss what makes an assignment "glow" and where an assignment needs to "grow."

Grows and Glows	
What Grows and Glows?	
Grows	*Glows*
Overall Thoughts and Recommendations	

Looking at Student Work

Looking in Depth at Student Work for Productive Struggle

	Response
Did the level of the task seem appropriate (not too easy, not too hard)?	
Did the student appear to struggle with his or her work?	
Would you say the student was successful with the task?	
How did you define success for this task?	
What recommendations would you make for improvement?	

A Final Note

Collaborating with other teachers is helpful when incorporating productive struggle in the classroom. In addition to co-creating activities, learning from each other can improve your practice. Finding time to effectively collaborate is challenging, but the benefits outweigh the disadvantages.

Points to Ponder

1. Which time management tip resonated with you? How can you implement it?
2. How can you and your fellow teachers improve collaboration?
3. Which of the activities for professional learning will you try in your school?

Continue the Learning

Use the QR Code to access videos for your own use or for group professional development.

Bibliography

Amidon, J., Monroe, A., Rock, D., & Cook, C. (2020). Shame, shame, go away: Fostering productive struggle with mathematics. *Kappa Delta Pi Record*, 56(2), 64–69.

Bates, B. (2023). *Learning theories simplified: . . . and how to apply them to teaching*. London: SAGE Publications Ltd.

Berger, R., Woodfin, L., & Vilen, A. (2016). *Learning that lasts*. San Francisco: Jossey Bass.

Blackburn, B. R. (2016). *Motivating struggling learners: Ten strategies for student success*. New York: Routledge.

Blackburn, B. R. (2019). *Rigor and differentiation in the classroom*. New York: Routledge.

Blackburn, B. R. (2020). *Rigor in the remote learning classroom*. New York: Routledge.

Blackburn, B. R. (2021). *Rigor in your classroom: A toolkit for teachers* (2nd ed.). New York: Routledge.

Blackburn, B. R. (2025). *Scaffolding for success*. New York: Routledge.

Blackburn, B. R. (2026a). *Rigor and assessment in the classroom*. New York: Routledge.

Blackburn, B. R. (2026b). *Rigor is not a four-letter word* (4th ed.). New York: Routledge.

Blackburn, B. R., & Armstrong, A. (2019). *Rigor in the 6-12 math and science classroom*. New York: Routledge.

Blackburn, B. R., & Armstrong, A. (2020). *Rigor in the K-5 math and science classroom*. New York: Routledge.

Blackburn, B. R., Armstrong, A., & Miles, M. (2018). Using writing to spark learning in math, science, and social studies. *ASCD Express*, 13(16). www.ascd.org/ascd-express/vol13/1316-blackburn.aspx?utm_source=ascdexpress&utm_medium=email&utm_campaign=Express%2D13%2D16

Blackburn, B. R., & Miles, M. (2019). *Rigor in the 6-12 language arts and social studies classroom*. New York: Routledge.

Blackburn, B. R., & Miles, M. (2020). *Rigor in the K-5 language arts and social studies classroom*. New York: Routledge.

Blackburn, B. R., & Witzel, B. (2018). *Rigor in the RTI/MTSS classroom*. New York: Routledge.

Blackburn, B. R., & Witzel, B. (2021). *Rigor for students with special needs* (2nd ed.). New York: Routledge.

Boryga, A. (2024, February 1). Helping young kids manage productive struggle. *Edutopia*. https://www.edutopia.org/article/helping-young-kids-manage-productive-struggle

Brown, P. C., Roediger, H. L., III, & McDaniel, M. A. (2014). *Make it stick: The science of successful learning*. The Belknap Press of Harvard University Press.

Bullmaster-Day, M. L. (2022). Key elements of productive struggle. *Waggle Blog (Renaissance Learning)*. https://blog.waggle.org/key-elements-of-productive-struggle

Bybee, R. W., Taylor, J. A., Gardner, A., Van Scotter, P., Carlson Powell, J., Westbrook, A., & Landes, N. (2006). *The BSCS 5E Instructional Model: Origins, effectiveness, and applications*. Colorado Springs, CO: BSCS.

Claxton, G. (2017). *The learning power approach: Teaching learners to teach themselves*. Thousand Oaks, CA: Corwin Press.

Colorado Department of Education (n.d.). *Taking action: Implementing effective mathematics teaching practices*. Colorado Dept. of Education. https://www.cde.state.co.us/comath/mathteachingpractice7

Corwin Authors. (2024, October). Why and how to encourage productive struggle. *Corwin Connect*. https://corwin-connect.com/2024/10/corwintalks-why-and-how-to-encourage-productive-struggle/

Costa, A. L., & Kallick, B. (2008). *Learning and leading with habits of mind: 16 essential characteristics for success*. Alexandria, VA: Association for Supervision and Curriculum Development.

Costa, A. L., & Kallick, B. (2014). *Dispositions: Reframing teaching and learning*. Thousand Oaks, CA: Corwin Press.

Cowen, E. (2016). Harnessing the power of productive struggle. *Edutopia*. https://www.edutopia.org/blog/harnessing-power-of-productive-struggle-ellie-cowen

Csikszentmihalyi, M. (2009). Flow. In S. Lopez (Ed.), *The encyclopedia of positive psychology* (pp. 394-400). Chichester: Blackwell Publishing Ltd.

Dean, C. B., Hubbell, E. R., Pitler, H., Stone, B., & Marzano, R. J. (2012). *Classroom instruction that works: Research-based strategies for increasing student achievement* (2nd ed.). ASCD.

Dinkmeyer, D., & Losoncy, L. (Ed.). (1992). *The encouragement book*. New York: Simon and Schuster.

DuFour, R., DuFour, R., Eaker, R., Many, T. W., & Mattos, M. (2016). *Learning by doing: A handbook for professional learning communities at work* (3rd ed.). Bloomington, IN: Solution Tree Press.

Dweck, C. S., & Elliott, E. S. (1983). Achievement motivation. In P. Mussen & E. M. Hetherington (Eds.), *Handbook of child psychology* (pp. 643–691). New York: Wiley.

Education Rickshaw. (2022, April 24). Do we want our students to struggle? *Education Rickshaw*. https://educationrickshaw.com/2022/04/24/do-we-want-our-students-to-struggle/

Elliott, E. S., & Dweck, C. S. (1988). Goals: An approach to motivation and achievement. *Journal of Personality and Social Psychology, 54*(1), 5–12.

ExploreLearning. (n.d.). What is productive struggle? *ExploreLearning*. https://www.explorelearning.com/resources/insights/productive-struggle

Ferlazzo, L. (2013). *Self-driven learning: Teaching strategies for student motivation*. New York: Routledge.

The GiST. (n.d.). Foster STEM dispositions. *The GiST*. Retrieved September 3, 2025, from https://www.thegist.edu.au/educators/create-inclusive-classrooms/talk-tools-build-stem-capital/foster-stem-dispositions/?utm_source=chatgpt.com

Goodwin, B., & Rouleau, K. (2019). *The new classroom instruction that works: The best research-based strategies for increasing student achievement*. Alexandria, VA: ASCD.

Grafwallner, P. J. (2021). *Not yet . . . and thats OK: How productive struggle fosters student learning*. Bloomington, IN: Solution Tree Press.

Hall, G. E., Quinn, L. F., & Gollnick, D. M. (Eds.). (2023). *The Wiley handbook of teaching and learning*. Hoboken, NJ: John Wiley & Sons, Inc.

Hattie, J., Fisher, D., Frey, N., & Almarode, J. (2024). *The illustrated guide to visible learning*. Thousand Oaks, CA: Corwin Press.

Hess, K. (2024). *Rigor by design, not chance: Deeper thinking through actionable instruction and assessment*. Thousand Oaks, CA: Corwin Press.

Hiebert, J., & Wearne, D. (2003). Developing understanding through problem solving. In H. L. Schoen (Ed.), *Teaching mathematics through problem solving: Grades 6 12* (pp. 3–13). Reston, VA: National Council of Teachers of Mathematics.

HMH Staff. (2022, June 6). What is productive struggle in the classroom? *HMH*. https://www.hmhco.com/blog/what-is-productive-struggle-in-the-classroom

Johnson, A. P. (2019). *Essential learning theories: Applications to authentic teaching and learning strategies*. Lanham, MD: Rowman & Littlefield.

Kapur, M. (2016). Examining productive failure, productive success, unproductive failure, and unproductive success in learning. *Educational Psychologist, 51*(2), 289–299.

Kennedy, M. (n.d.). The key to understanding productive struggle in games. *MIND Research Institute*. https://blog.mindresearch.org/blog/the-key-to-understanding-productive-struggle-in-games-is-here

Kettler, R. J. (2012). Testing accommodations: Theory and research to inform practice. *International Journal of Disability, Development and Education, 5*, 53–66.

Khalil, I., Al-Otaibi, A., Almughyriah, S., & Almalky, M. (2025). How do students evaluate their teachers' support for productive struggle in learning mathematics? *Cogent Education, 12*(1).

Marshall, J. C. (2019). *Rise to the challenge*. Alexandria, VA: Association for Supervision and Curriculum Development.

Martin, K. (2019, November 3). The power of productive struggle. *Katie Martin*. https://katiemartin.com/2019/11/03/the-power-of-productive-struggle/

Marzano, R. J. (Ed.). (2010). *On excellence in teaching* (10th ed.). Solution Tree Press.

Marzano, R. J., Pickering, D. J., & Pollock, J. E. (2001). *Classroom instruction that works*. Alexandria, VA: Association for Supervision and Curriculum Development.

McDonnell, L. M., McLaughlin, M. J., & Morison, P. (1997). *Educating one and all: Students with disabilities and standards-based reform*. National Academy Press.

McDowell, M. (2024). *Rigor redefined: Ten teaching habits for surface, deep, and transfer learning*. Bloomington, IN: Solution Tree Press.

National Council of Teachers of Mathematics (NCTM). (2017). *Enhancing classroom practice with research behind principles in action*. Reston, VA: Author.

Newmann, F. M., Carmichael, D., & King, M. B. (2016). *Authentic intellectual work: Improving teaching for rigorous learning*. Thousand Oaks, CA: Corwin Press.

Nottingham, J. (2016). *Challenging learning: Theory, effective practice and lesson ideas to create optimal learning in the classroom* (2nd ed.). Routledge.

Nottingham, J. (2017). *Challenging learning through feedback: How to guide your students to be more critical, creative, and independent learners*. Corwin.

Nottingham, J. (2017). *The learning challenge*. Thousand Oaks, CA: Corwin Press.

Nottingham, J. (2024). *Teach brilliantly: Small shifts that lead to big gains in student learning*. Bloomington, IN: Solution Tree Press.

Park, J., Starett, E., Chen, Y-C., & Jordan, M. (2024). Facilitating productive struggle in science education. *The Mathematics Enthusiast*. https://scholarworks.umt.edu/tme/vol21/iss1/7

Paurowski, M., Glassmeyer, D., Kim, J., & Id-Deen, L. (2024). Struggling as part of success: International Baccalaureate students' productive struggle is strongly correlated to mathematical achievement. *International Journal of Mathematical Education in Science and Technology*.

Ph.D. Science. (2022, December 9). How do you support students through productive struggle? *Great Minds*. https://greatminds.org/

Pink, D. (2009). *Drive: The surprising truth about what motivates us*. New York: Penguin Books.

Ritchart, R. (2002). *Intellectual character: What it is, why it matters, and how to get it*. San Francisco, CA: Jossey-Bass.

Ritchart, R. (2015). *Creating cultures of thinking: The 8 forces we must master to truly transform our schools*. San Francisco, CA: Jossey-Bass.

Ritchart, R. (2023). *Cultures of thinking in action: 10 mindsets to transform our teaching and students learning*. Jossey-Bass.

SanGiovanni, J., Katt, J., & Dykema, C. (2020). *Productive math struggle: A 6-point action plan for fostering perseverance*. Corwin Mathematics.

Schwartz, K. (2015, August 4). Seeing struggling math learners as 'sense makers,' not 'mistake makers'. *Mind/Shift (KQED)*. https://www.kqed.org/mindshift/40537/seeing-struggling-math-learners-as-sense-makers-not-mistake-makers

Settle, S. A., & Milich, R. (1999). Social persistence following failure in boys and girls with LD. *Journal of Learning Disabilities, 32*, 201–212.

Sibberson, F., Szymusiak, K., & Koch, L. (2008). *Beyond leveled books: Supporting early and transitional readers in grades K5* (2nd ed.). Stenhouse Publishers.

Spencer, J. (2017). *Making learning flow*. Bloomington, IL: Solution Tree.

Sriram, R. (2020). The neuroscience behind productive struggle. *Edutopia*. https://www.edutopia.org/article/neuroscience-behind-productive-struggle/

ST Math Staff. (n.d.). The importance of productive struggle. *ST Math*. https://www.stmath.com/productive-struggle-math-rigor

STEMscopes Staff. (n.d.). 5 Reasons the productive struggle belongs in STEM. *Accelerate Learning Blog*. https://blog.acceleratelearning.com/5-reasons-the-productive-struggle-belongs-in-stem

Thibodeau, T. (2024). How to harness productive struggle. *Novak Education*. https://www.novakeducation.com/blog/how-to-harness-productive-struggle

Thibodeau, T. (n.d.-b). *What is productive struggle*. https://www.novakeducation.com/blog/how-to-harness-productive-struggle

Tomlinson, C. A., & Moon, T. R. (2013). *Assessment and student success in a differentiated classroom*. Alexandria, VA: ASCD.

VanLehn, K., Burkhardt, H., Cheema, S., Kang, S., Pead, D., Schoenfeld, A., & Wetzel, J. (2019). Can an orchestration system increase collaborative, productive struggle in teaching-by-eliciting classrooms? *Interactive Learning Environments*. https://doi.org/10.1080/10494820.2019.1611657

Vygotsky, L. S. (1978). *Mind in society: The development of higher psychological processes.* Cambridge, MA: Harvard University Press.

Wagner, T. (2008). *The global achievement gap: Why even our best schools dont teach the new survival skills our children needand what we can do about it.* New York: Basic Books.

Warshauer, H. K. (2015). Strategies to support productive struggle. *Mathematics Teaching in the Middle School, 20*(7), 390–393.

Wiederhold, C. (1995). *The Q-Matrix: Cooperative Learning and Critical Thinking.* San Juan Capistrano, CA : Kagan Cooperative Learning.

Williamson, R., & Blackburn, B. (2016). *The principalship from A to Z* (2nd ed.). Routledge.

Williamson, R., & Blackburn, B. (2019). *Rigor in your school: A toolkit for leaders* (2nd ed.). New York: Routledge.

Williamson, R., & Blackburn, B. (2020). *7 strategies for improving your school.* New York: Routledge.

Williamson, R., & Blackburn, B. (2024). *Improving teacher morale and motivation.* New York: Routledge.

Witherell, J. (n.d.). Productive struggle. *Goyen Education.* https://www.goyen.io/blog/productivestruggle

Young, J. R., Bevan, D., & Sanders, M. (2024). How productive is the productive struggle? Lessons learned from a scoping review. *International Journal of Education in Mathematics, Science, and Technology.* https://doi.org/10.46328/ijemst.3364

Young, L. A. J. (2024, October 1). Thriving in the zone of productive struggle. *ASCD.* https://www.ascd.org/blogs/thriving-in-the-zone-of-productive-struggle

For Product Safety Concerns and Information please contact our EU
representative GPSR@taylorandfrancis.com
Taylor & Francis Verlag GmbH, Kaufingerstraße 24, 80331 München, Germany

www.ingramcontent.com/pod-product-compliance
Lightning Source LLC
Chambersburg PA
CBHW080733300426
44114CB00019B/2578